Praise for *New Life through Shared Ministry*

"The new life that comes from a respectful and healthy shared ministry system is felt by all: the congregation, the individual, the ministries, and those they serve. Through this book you get the insight of someone who has done this work, been in many other settings, and listened to other practitioners share their experiences."
—Jan Frederickson, director of shared ministry, Nativity Lutheran Church

"Judy Urban tackles what can be a sometimes 'mushy' and confusing aspect of congregational life—member engagement or volunteer involvement. She not only offers a comprehensive and thorough roadmap for growing a culture of shared ministry in your congregation, but clearly delineates the benefits of doing so."
—Sally Carlson-Bancroft, volunteer support, The Basilica of Saint Mary

"Church people often ask me, 'So, just how do you get 3,000 volunteer ministers involved?' Sometimes I give a short answer and sometimes a longer answer, but there is no magic answer. If you read Judy Urban's thoughtful book and work through her steps, you too will have the answer. Soon others will be asking you, 'Just how do you get all those volunteers ministers involved?'"
—Barb Orzechowski, pastoral associate for shared ministry, Church of St. John Neumann

"In *New Life through Shared Ministry*, Judy Urban has provided congregations a masterpiece both for revitalizing their congregations and for being faithful to God's call to all people to be ministers in the church and the world. Judy's strength as an author emerges from the wide variety of perspectives she brings to shared ministry—as a former director of shared ministry, as a leader in groups of shared ministry professionals, as one who has trained many in introducing risk management procedures in churches, as an expert in how a shared ministry director works with other church staff members, and as a shared ministry educator and consultant with many congregations. If your church wants to be successful in shared ministry, Judy is just the person whose guidance you will need to get there."

—Jean Morris Trumbauer, director, Doctor of Ministry Program, United Theological Seminary

"If you build it they will come! Building a culture of shared ministry in a congregation is the key to recruiting and retaining volunteers effectively and essential for engaging members as partners in the work of the church. *New Life through Shared Ministry* is an invaluable resource to help a congregation get started. It is a comprehensive manual that provides the rationale, framework and tools for building a culture in which everyone shares in the ministry. *New Life through Shared Ministry* has provided me with many fresh ideas and new challenges that will keep my shared ministry committee busy for a long time."

—Marion Clark, director of shared ministry, St. Bartholomew Catholic Faith Community

New Life
through
Shared Ministry

New Life
through
Shared Ministry

Moving from Volunteering to Mission

Judith A. Urban

The Alban Institute
Herndon, VA
www.alban.org

The Alban Institute
2121 Cooperative Way, Suite 100
Herndon, VA 20171

Library of Congress Cataloging-in-Publication Data
Urban, Judith A.
 The new life through shared ministry : moving from volunteering to mission / Judith A. Urban.
      pages cm
 Includes bibliographical references and index.
 ISBN 978-1-56699-435-4 (alk. paper)
 1. Cooperative ministry. 2. Lay ministry. 3. Church work. I. Title.
 BV675.5.U73 2013
 253--dc23
                                    2012040327

13   14   15   16   17   VG   5   4   3   2   1

Contents

Foreword

Judy Urban's book, *New Life through Shared Ministry: Moving from Volunteering to Mission*, has been unfolding for seventeen years. Judy's professional work in this field began when she served as pastoral associate of shared ministry for the large Roman Catholic parish where I was then pastor. During her six years in that position, she helped transform an active volunteer ministry into a truly shared ministry, one that involved many more members than most parishes experienced and saw members eagerly stepping forward to take responsibility for leading the parish's ministries. In the eleven years since we worked together, Judy has consulted with dozens of congregations throughout the United States, sharing her skills and wisdom and helping them to change the culture of their faith community and unleash members' many gifts for ministry.

One of the many reasons I have so appreciated Judy's work is that her clear, practical roadmap for implementing shared ministry in day-to-day congregational life is consistent with my own theology of ministry. It has taken me a long time to recognize that the way I look at ministry is directly related to the way I understand God. For much of my life, the Trinity was a theological or intellectual puzzle to be marveled at as a mystery of faith but with little importance for the shape of Church life and ministry. The Trinity was a doctrine to believe, not a dynamic reality to be lived. Western Christianity affirms that God is Father, Son, and Holy Spirit. Yet we often simply pray to God, leaving out reference to a Person of the Trinity, or we pray to our favorite Person of the Trinity, without denying the others. The Holy Spirit is often called the forgotten Person of the Trinity. The Trinity is more evident in Eastern Christianity where the Father, Son, and Holy Spirit are invoked over and over again in a seamless litany of prayer in the liturgy. Assigning the Trinity to the realm of an impossible theological puzzle is not our only difficulty in thinking about God. Too often Christian piety has imagined God as a lonely old man in the sky. What happens to communities and church leaders when they see the God they represent as a solitary, celestial figure overseeing and controlling the universe?

In creating the human race, Genesis hints at the truth about the nature of God that will not be clarified for centuries. God said: "Let us make man in our image, after our likeness. Let them have dominion over the fish of the sea, the birds of the air, and the cattle, and over all the wild animals and all the creatures that crawl on the ground. God created man in his image; in the divine image he created him; male and female he created them." A little later God is pictured saying "It is not good for the man to be alone. I will make a suitable partner for him." Could it be that it is not good for the man to be alone because human beings were made in the image and likeness of God? Partnership belongs to human nature because without partnership we would not be able to mirror the image of a God who is in fact Trinity.

As Trinity, three equal divine Persons participate in diverse ways in one and the same saving mission. In God there is common mission and collaboration in the shared work of creation and salvation. Salvation happens through the interaction of three Divine Persons. While each of the three Persons is certainly God, the godhead—or what we mean by "God"—is a wholeness or communion rooted in the relationship of the Persons to one another. Another way of saying the same thing is captured in the book of John: "God is love. Whoever lives in love lives in God, and God in them" (4:16). Grace is a participation in the life of God. Therefore grace is communion in Divine love and in a Trinitarian way of acting.

The Catechism of the Catholic Church says, "In virtue of their rebirth in Christ there exists among all the Christian faithful a true equality with regard to dignity and the activity whereby all cooperate in the building up of the Body of Christ in accord with each one's own condition and function. The very differences which the Lord has willed to put between the members of his body serve its unity and mission. For "in the Church there is diversity of ministry but unity of mission (871-3). Therefore the Church is a community of equal persons participating in diverse ways in one common mission. The mission of the Church is accomplished only through the inter-action of all its members. Just as the Father is the source of authority in the Trinity, there is also a source of authority in the Church. The Son is the faithful response in the Trinity. There is also faithful response in the Church. The Holy Spirit is the bond of love and creative power in the Trinity. Love and empowerment are also embodied in the ministries and charisms of the Church. Yet none of these are the prerogative of one person standing outside of the communion of the whole, either in the Trinity or in the Church. The Church comes to fullness only through the collaboration of many roles and ministries in one mission—in imitation of the Trinity. Of course, imitation is far too weak a word to reflect the relationship between the Trinity and the life and ministry of the Church. The Church is a communion of equal persons collaborating in diverse ways in a common mission because the Church participates in the life of the Trinity. The grace that we experience is the grace of the Trinity; it is not the life of the solitary old man looking down and controlling the universe from heaven. When we and our communities do not share ministry and pride ourselves in acting like the boss or the lone ranger, it is appropriate to ask questions about the "god" we worship and in whose image we are shaping our lives.

Jesus prayed for a unity among his followers that would be so profound it would mirror the life of God: "My prayer is not for them alone. I pray also for those who will believe in me through their message, that all of them may be one, Father, just as you are in me and I am in you. May they also be in us so that the world may believe that you have sent me. I have given them the glory that you gave me, that they may be one as we are one—I in them and you in me—so that they may be brought to complete unity.

Then the world will know that you sent me and have loved them even as you have loved me" (John 17:20-23).

As the pastor of a large suburban parish, it would be impossible to minister to the needs of our community alone, to say nothing about participating in the worldwide mission of the Jesus Christ. My reason for embracing shared ministry whole-heartedly involves much more than being more effective or the impossibility of ministering to this community as the long ranger. I believe that shared ministry flows from our sharing in the life of the Trinity. Shared ministry expresses the very nature of the church. We were created for partnership by the Triune God. Partnership with God with one another is the path to Christian holiness. Shared ministry is about living in God and God living in us.

Congregational leaders whose theological sympathies align with my own will find *New Life through Shared Ministry* is an indispensable tool for helping members grow in their understanding of ministry and inviting them to share their gifts for service both in the congregation and in the communities beyond.

Fr. Robert M. Schwartz
Our Lady of Grace Parish
Edina, Minnesota

Preface

Shared ministry is a term used to describe a process and system for effectively involving lay members of a congregation in its mission and work. Based on inviting members of the church to serve using their unique gifts, interests, and passions, this book presents a "quick-start" method for beginning to build such a shared ministry system. This comprehensive guide is based on the consulting, training, and planning that I have done with many congregations during the past twelve years; my own experience of building a shared ministry system in a church; and the many educational opportunities in the field of volunteer management I have taken advantage of over the years. Most significantly, I based my study and practice on the work of Jean Morris Trumbauer, whose expertise in the field of church volunteer management is recognized nationally. Her book *Sharing the Ministry: A Practical Guide for Transforming Volunteers into Ministers* is the de facto standard reference work in the field.[1] I owe much of my knowledge and success in my work to her materials, training, and mentoring over the years.

In my work as a consultant to churches, after the group I am working with experiences initial excitement over the possibilities, I often hear the lament, "It's all so overwhelming. Where do I start?" Faith communities want a clear, succinct outline for building such a system, and this book presents a sequence for beginning the building process. It offers many tips and suggestions for ways to create the building blocks that will bring about positive change. The goal is to assist you in transforming your church into one where as many people as possible are invited into volunteer ministry, where people are matched according to their gifts and interests with ministry opportunities, and where they are offered support, training, and appreciation.

I have written this book with the assumption that the congregation has within it an identified champion of the shared ministry concept. This person could be any one or a combination of the following:

- a paid staff member working full time on the task
- a paid staff member working part time with shared ministry, possibly blending it with other staff responsibilities
- an unpaid volunteer working in a quasi-staff position
- a team of volunteers with passion for the topic

In any case the congregation needs some group or individual whose job it is to focus energy and planning on building a shared ministry system. When it becomes everyone's task, it is nobody's task.

I will present my ideas from the perspective of a paid staff person having the role of director of shared ministry within the congregation. However, I will try to indicate how a part-time staff member or volunteer committee could accomplish the same functions. Always keep in mind, however, that the less time the director of shared ministry has to spend on building a shared ministry system and its related responsibilities, the longer it will take to achieve that goal. In addition, the less attention and focus is given to the project, the longer it will take to bring about any depth and breadth of change within the culture, thereby lessening the likelihood that such change lasts. The shallower and narrower the shared ministry culture, the more easily it can be lost with a change in leadership, staffing, or priorities.

I have experience with all these models. I have worked as a member of a volunteer shared ministry committee with only a staff liaison, who is not a shared ministry director, acting as a conduit of information and support between congregation leaders and the committee. So I have firsthand knowledge of the joys of this approach and the abilities of such a group to move forward; I also have an awareness of the ultimate limitations and frustrations of utilizing this model alone to create a shared ministry culture. In my consulting work I have seen how a part-time staff member can effectively build a shared ministry system, but I have also seen the limitations of this model due to time and energy constraints. Finally, I have seen and directly experienced how much progress can be made when there is full-time focus on the task. The plan that will bring the quickest and longest-lasting results is for someone to work full time on all aspects of a shared ministry system and in partnership with a shared ministry team that builds ownership, offers support, and provides a wider variety of ideas.

Although I will present a specific sequence based on my experience working with many churches, keep in mind that each congregation is unique. The sequence can be changed, to a certain extent, to meet the needs of the particular faith community.

Acknowledgments

I would like to thank Jean Trumbauer—my teacher, mentor, colleague, and friend—for introducing me to shared ministry, helping me learn about building the system, giving me practical advice and support throughout my professional career in the field, trusting me enough to work with her on a collegial basis, and honoring me by turning over her consulting business to me when she moved into another stage in her life.

I would like to thank all my colleagues in the field who have given me support and encouragement throughout the years and from whom I have learned so much about working with congregations. There are so many that it would be difficult to name them all. It was their interest and encouragement that energized me to write this book. I also wish to thank the staff of St. John Neumann Catholic Church, particularly Father Bob Schwartz, former pastor, who hired me and gave me the opportunity to build a shared ministry system from the ground up.

I wish to thank my husband, Roger, who spent countless hours reading my early drafts and making excellent suggestions, and who has uncomplainingly given me the months of time I needed to spend working on the manuscript.

I wish to thank Beth Gaede, my editor, as well as Andrea Lee, copy editor, and Lauren Belen of Alban, who turned a novice attempt at writing a book into a work that became good enough to publish.

Finally, I humbly praise and thank God, who has nudged me along this path from the beginning, who blessed me with so many opportunities to learn and grow, and who instilled in me the gifts necessary to follow the plan God had for my life.

CHAPTER 1

What Is Shared Ministry Anyway?

S hared ministry refers to what some people would call *volunteerism* in everyday life—activities such as helping out in a child's classroom, working on a political campaign, giving time delivering flowers in a hospital, or doing unpaid work for a charitable organization. The term *service* is often used to refer to the work of volunteerism. The term *shared ministry* refers to a particular type of volunteering—all the many ways members of a congregation serve their faith community and the wider community. The statements typically made about shared ministry are such things as "People are invited into ministry, they share their gifts in performing their ministry, and the congregation has many ministry opportunities available to its members." We will see that shared ministry has certain characteristics not always present in non-faith-based organizations. Shared ministry refers to both a concept and a system.

Shared Ministry as Concept

Shared ministry is based on the concept that all believers are called to participate in the work of the church, in bringing the good news of God's saving grace to the whole world. Each Christian denomination bases this understanding of such a call in Scripture, the teachings of its leaders, and doctrines born of tradition. All teach that the individual believer is called to participate in growing the reign of God in every age.

Our call to shared ministry is part of our membership in a congregation. All members, not just the ordained and the paid staff, are called to service—invited to contribute their gifts, energy, and passions to this overarching purpose. Hence the term *shared*. A shared ministry system is based on a core value that participation in the ministry of the church is the right and responsibility of each member.

Shared Ministry as System

Shared ministry is also a system of many interrelated parts that work together to bring the concept into reality. Shared ministry is not a program. It is a way of being church together. It creates a distinctive church culture. The system enables people to discover their own gifts; to match them with appropriate ministry opportunities; to be supported, trained, affirmed, and appreciated in their ministry; and to grow to spiritual maturity through that ministry.

Based on both the work of Jean Morris Trumbauer in her foundational book *Sharing the Ministry: A Practical Guide for Transforming Volunteers into Ministers*[1] and the basic principles of volunteerism used in the nonprofit arena, this system can be defined and organized so that it can be learned and used. It is the foundation for building members' experience of life in their church, a life that participates fully and actively in fulfilling the mission of the church. Jean Trumbauer defines shared ministry this way:

> Shared ministry lives out the affirmation that God calls all people to ministry. As members of faith communities, we are invited to serve together in a spirit of mutuality as partners. Working collaboratively, we strive to discover, develop, engage, and support the gifts of each person and, as responsible stewards, to

participate in God's ongoing creative and restoring activity in our communities and the world.[2]

Shared ministry is based on each individual's gifts—identifying them, matching them to appropriate ministry opportunities, helping the gifts to flourish and contribute to God's plan for God's people. Because these gifts have been freely given to us, we are to be stewards or caretakers of them. We are not the originators of our gifts. They are merely loaned to us to be used for our lifetime. As we use our gifts we are doing ministry alongside others who are using theirs. Each person's role complements the gifts of others. We work together toward a common goal.

Theology of Gifts

As Christians, the theological basis for shared ministry is the belief that we are an incarnational people. We believe that God sent God's Son as the body-and-blood, fleshly proof of God's passionate participation in human life. Furthermore, we believe that God continues to become flesh in our lives. God lives in each one of us. God is active in each member of our parish and indeed in every human being. God chose us, redeemed us, and loved us into God's own life of grace.

We participate in this incarnational experience by becoming partners with God and with each other in carrying out God's plan. This partnership with each other consists of building relationships and sharing a commitment to the vision and work given to us by our Creator. We treat each other with mutual trust; we share our gifts in common effort. In shared ministry we respect and affirm the unique but equal roles each member brings to the effort. We honor diversity, and we value each person's individual contribution to the whole.

Jesus is our model for a life of self-giving. Jesus always showed respect and affirmation for each individual he came in contact with. He called a diverse group of individuals to be his followers: fishermen, tax collectors, soldiers, and women. But Jesus spoke humbly about the source of his mission: "I do nothing on my own, but I say only what the Father taught me" (John 8:28). Jesus was sent from God the Father to show God's love for the world by offering himself up in reparation for our sins. That was his mission. We are sent to spread the good news of God's love for all people to the entire world: "As you sent me into the world, so I sent them into the world" (John 17:18).

A theology of gifts undergirds a shared ministry system—a system based upon the belief that God has blessed every individual with many gifts. Shared ministry looks at gifts from a holistic viewpoint, as being composed of more than just the individual's special skills and abilities. The term *gifts* also includes such things as one's life experiences, personality type, preferences for ways of learning, preferred patterns for interacting with other individuals, key motivations, work environment needs, physical attributes, spiritual heritage, strengths and weaknesses, dreams and desires, emotions and values. In short, everything that makes us who we are as individuals comprises our gift "package."[3]

Motivational gifts are one type of gift. Life experiences are another type of gift. Congregations will mean different things when they use the term *gifts*. Some congregations focus on a group of gifts they call "spiritual" gifts. These congregations define spiritual gifts as those intended by God to be used specifically in building up God's church. Other congregations do not make this distinction. A case could be made that because all gifts come from God, every gift is a spiritual gift.

Individuals may decide to use their gifts within a congregation's ministries or simply share their gifts out in the community in ways not specifically connected to their congregation. I will use the term *shared ministry* to apply to the ways people contribute their gifts in any volunteer service performed under the auspices of a congregation. This service may be to the surrounding community or strictly to the congregation itself. If it is authorized by a congregation, I call it shared ministry because it is service being shared with the ordained, paid staff and members of the faith community. Volunteer service performed on one's own or under the auspices of organizations not directly connected to the congregation may qualify as ministry because it serves others. But because the service, worthy as it may be, lacks this connection to the congregation, it is not shared ministry as I choose to use the term.

However you define the word *gifts*, the shared ministry system is based on recognition that these gifts come from a loving God. The system enables members of a congregation to discover and use these gifts.

One can spend many hours studying the theological underpinnings and principles related to shared ministry. This is a fruitful endeavor and one I would encourage, although it is beyond the scope of this book.

Changing the Culture

In my experience, it is when people encounter the system of shared ministry within their congregation that the system truly becomes real in their hearts and minds. Any congregation that begins building a shared ministry system experiences some confusion and uncertainty about exactly what supposed to be doing and why. Only by going through the process of building the components do the shared ministry team and the members of the church fully realize what shared ministry is. Building a shared ministry system changes a church culture.

One definition of *culture* is the shared beliefs and values of a group—the customs, practices, and social behavior of a particular nation or group. The term can also be used to identify the particular place, class, or time to which a people belong. Every congregation already has a culture—the way things are done, the values important to the group, the unique organization of practices and processes, communication methods and links, reactions to those who are not part of that congregation, and power structures.

Shared ministry enables the congregation to add to or adapt the existing culture and change it into something new. It brings new life to the ministry of the people of a faith community. It invites members into the mission of the congregation and facilitates their participation. Shared ministry enlivens faith and energizes commitment.

A changed culture does not happen overnight or with just one attempt to put one of the components in place. This new culture slowly emerges, bit by bit, as church members experience doing things in a new way or from a different perspective. Few members will be able to articulate what shared ministry is all about in the beginning. Rather, their understanding comes from experiencing the components as they are created and brought into the life of the congregation.

Components of a Shared Ministry System

To follow the process I am outlining in this book, you will need a basic understanding of how systems function. In a system, each component affects and is affected by every other component. When you change one part of the system, you will necessarily create ripples of change throughout the rest of the system. The changes can have negative or beneficial effects. A positive movement in a key component can create significant changes for the good, often showing surprising acceleration instead of the anticipated slow, gradual progress. At a certain point a critical mass is reached and there is an explosion of energy, understanding, and participation. The intent of this book is to guide the process for putting the components of the shared ministry system in place.

Figure 1.1. Components of a Shared Ministry System[4]

Figure 1.1 represents the shared ministry system as a series of globes. These globes are configured in a circle (imagine a mobile), with each globe representing one of the system components. Each globe slightly overlaps those on either side of it. In addition, as with a mobile, when the globes are in motion, each one can touch every other globe in the mobile, creating a rippling effect.

The components consist of the following:

Planning
Discovering gifts
Designing
Recruiting
Interviewing
Matching

Training
Supervising
Supporting
Evaluating
Managing data
Managing risk

Readers will notice that the component of managing risk does not appear on the globes in the diagram. Since Trumbauer's book was published, this component has become exceedingly important for congregations, ensuring safety for both those being served and the volunteer ministers. Therefore I have added it to the list of components.

Many of these elements can also be found in non-faith-based volunteer management systems. They are part of the professional approach to involving volunteers in nonprofit organizations. What shared ministry does is place these elements into a faith-based context and add the theological understanding that each individual is called to use his or her unique gifts in the service of building God's world.

All key leaders in the church need to have an understanding of these elements so that they can follow the work of the shared ministry team and director, understand why the elements are important, and support their implementation.

COMPONENTS DESCRIBED

The *planning* component refers in part to the initial processes of studying the current culture in your congregation. Planners seek to discover what elements of a shared ministry system already exist and do not need to be reinvented. They identify the current strengths of the culture, what components are missing or insufficient, the level of understanding of each component's importance, and the amount of support the director and team are likely to receive. Based on this assessment, the planning committee makes strategic decisions about which components to concentrate on first and how to move forward. Included in planning is also the work of identifying, recruiting, and forming a shared ministry team and creating a written plan that is updated on a regular basis.

Discovering gifts involves building processes that enable and encourage members to learn what their gifts for ministry are so that they can use them to more effectively participate in the mission of their parish and in many different situations throughout their lives. These processes include such things as gift-discovery classes, gift inventories, gift databanks, and one-on-one coaching. Chapter 9 explores in greater depth how the concept of gifts can be naturally woven into the process of building a shared ministry culture.

Designing starts with analyzing how the existing ministries are functioning. The committee asks such questions as, Where are the sticking points that make it difficult for members to participate? Where could a change in how the ministry is organized and works better meet the needs of today's volunteer minister? What new ministry opportunities need to be created? What will ministries look like in this new shared ministry culture? How can meaningful position descriptions be written for each ministry? After looking at these questions, the next step is to work collaboratively with stakeholders to create new ministries or update existing ones, taking into account the needs and lifestyles of today's congregation members. Position descriptions may need to be rewritten or tweaked to better appeal to potential members of the ministries.

Recruiting deals with the methods used to invite people into the ministry of the church. What techniques and practices—both effective and ineffective—are currently being used? What changes can be introduced to improve these processes? How can the system be designed so people don't fall through the cracks?

Interviewing refers to the discussions that take place at key times in the life of an individual's ministry in the church. These conversations may focus on gifts discovery; welcoming and exploring shared ministry with new members; assisting people in finding their place in particular ministries; recruiting specific people for particular positions in a ministry, such as leadership; screening potential ministry candidates; supervisory issues; and exit interviews for those leaving a particular ministry position.

Matching is a process that enables the individual to find a comfortable fit between his or her gifts, interests, available time, and current ministry opportunities.

Training has to do with examining current training practices and designing excellent learning experiences for volunteer ministers. This helps people perform their work well, helps them grow in their spiritual lives, and encourages the transfer of skills and knowledge from ministry into other areas of daily life.

Supervising promotes a partnership between the volunteer minister and the accountable leader or staff person. It involves helping the individual to be most effective in his or her chosen ministry.

Supporting involves providing practical assistance for volunteer ministers to accomplish their tasks by removing barriers and providing material resources, information, and orientation. It also helps individuals feel that their gifts and unique identities are fully respected and appreciated.

Evaluating offers opportunities for volunteer ministers to assess, individually and as a ministry group, how they can improve their own performance and the effectiveness of their ministry. It also encourages the committee or team to examine the internal group dynamics in the ministry and the level of satisfaction ministry members experience as they carry out their tasks.

Managing data means capturing information and maintaining records relating to individuals' participation in specific ministries, completion and results of screening processes, attendance at training opportunities, leadership positions, gifts, and other important data.

Managing risks refers to creating policies and procedures for keeping volunteer ministers, those they serve, and the congregation itself free from harm.

The Synchronicity of the System

Synchronicity refers to the influence for good each component of the shared ministry system brings to bear on every other component. When things are in sync with each other, all parts harmoniously contribute to and support each other to improve the working of the entire system. When things are out of sync with each other, the system is less effective in reaching the desired outcomes. In systems that are out of sync, we find gaps between components, communication problems, unnecessary duplications, and components working against each other. We can easily find many examples of how the components of the system affect each other.

I worked with one congregation where a dedicated usher remarked that in the fifteen years he had stood next to the pastor at the back of church each Sunday morning, never once had that pastor acknowledged his presence and ministry with even so much as a "Good morning." The ushers were having a lot of trouble getting younger members to join their ministry. Many of the current ushers had been serving in this role for twenty-five years or longer. They were growing weary, and several of the current ushers were in ill health. Yet no one could be found to take their places.

Word had gotten out that the job of usher was a thankless one in which no one recognized or affirmed the usher's presence much less showed appreciation for the ministry performed. Ushers did not have the sense that they were participating as colleagues in the mission of that church. Because of the lack of a relationship between the pastor and the ushers, the ushers themselves had no model for fostering fellowship among their own members. Thus volunteers carried out their work in a joyless, isolated fashion—a real turnoff to younger generations looking for connection. The poor support component had all sorts of negative impacts on the effectiveness of the recruitment component.

In another instance, no attempt was made to match the volunteer minister's gifts with the ministry best suited to those gifts. Warm bodies were plugged into holes in ministry areas with no thought to finding a good fit. In this church people understood that when someone came forward and expressed a desire to get involved, he or she could end up anywhere there was a current vacancy. It did not matter if people were interested in a different ministry or if a different ministry would allow them to make the better use of their gifts.

A variation of this problem occurred in a church that operated with the theory that everyone takes turns being a member of the leadership council, becoming the chair of a committee, acting as liaison to each of the standing committees, taking the notes, doing the scheduling, or any one of a myriad of tasks. The general attitude seemed to be that people were like interchangeable building blocks that could be plugged in pretty much anywhere. The fact that all kinds of round pegs were forced into square holes was frustrating to all involved. This, in turn, generated numerous difficulties as leaders of ministries and paid staff struggled to supervise effectively, to evaluate accomplishments, and to provide appropriate training. Not surprisingly, recruitment attempts were generally not successful as people feared putting themselves in a position where they could be working in such an unrewarding capacity. The lack of a matching component had a negative effect on the supervision, evaluating, training, and recruitment components.

Synchronicity can also bring about positive changes for a faith community, as the following examples illustrate. One congregation worked hard to create a database, ensuring that no one who signed up to participate in any ministry would be overlooked. The success of this plan contributed to a dramatic increase in the number of people committing during the annual fall recruitment to serve in various ministries. Word got out through the positive experiences members had that this church really cared about its volunteer ministers. No one was ignored or left dangling when they communicated a desire to participate. This is an example of the positive impact the database component had on the recruitment component.

Another congregation had difficulty recruiting and retaining teachers of religious education for school-age children. The congregation devised a comprehensive training program for the teachers. All new teachers attended a daylong workshop where they learned classroom management, including how to encourage discussion and participation, discipline measures, risk management procedures, and screening requirements for all those working with children or vulnerable adults. They were given an outline of the classes for the entire year with step-by-step explanations on how to present material as well as background reading on each topic.

Each new teacher was paired with an experienced one for the first year. The new teacher gradually began presenting some of the class material. The staff supervisor met with these pairs several times a year to explore how things were going, offer advice, and troubleshoot problems. Once a quarter, all the teachers, new and experienced, met together for a workshop and time to connect with each other.

At the end of the instruction year, the teachers were treated to a dinner, and representative staff members and parents had the opportunity to express their appreciation for their hard work. All the teachers were asked to fill out a form evaluating their own performance and how they had grown in their faith from their experiences throughout the year. They were also asked to evaluate how well they had been prepared to teach and to reflect on the support they had received from colleagues and staff members. The religious education staff member and leadership team used this information to make needed changes for the next year. Because of this system, the turnover among teachers was low. When an experienced teacher left the ministry, teachers who had been mentored were available to take over a class. The training, support, supervision, and evaluation components positively affected recruitment.

In addition, through a gifts discovery and matching interview, the shared ministry staff person identified a congregation member with the gift for curriculum design and development. Using her gifts, the member rewrote the curriculums for several grades. The new curriculums made it much easier for the teachers to learn how to teach some difficult topics. This in turn encouraged the teachers to continue the next year. In this case, then, we can see the gifts-discovery processes and the interviewing process affecting the training, support, and recruitment components.

The beauty of the shared ministry system is that the avenues for positive synchronicity are built into the system itself. Congregations are virtually assured that if they improve one of the components, they will automatically realize gains in one or more of the other components. The components are that closely connected.

The point of all these examples is that the mission of the church can be dramatically affected for good or ill depending on whether attention is paid to building each of the components and constantly improving upon them. All the shared ministry components facilitate the outreach and unique work God gives each congregation. They provide the underpinnings, the supporting network that allows true excellence and effectiveness in the ministry of the people of God.

CHAPTER 2

Why Shared Ministry?

H aving read a description of what shared ministry is, you might still ask several important questions: Why should our congregation attempt to build such a system? What does shared ministry offer that is so different from the way most of us do things now? What issues and problems does it address? Will it make a significant difference to our mission and church life? What do we stand to gain from making a serious attempt to build such a system? Is it worth investing time, energy, and money?

Shared Ministry Is Good for All Congregations

Shared ministry creates a congregational culture in which each member is invited to participate in ministry and helped to do so through proven systems and processes. It brings new life and energy to the congregation. Members learn that all people have gifts and all are called to use them in building the reign of God. Shared ministry creates the environment in which this can actually happen.

The shared ministry process when fully implemented yields numerous benefits. Many more people are sharing the tasks of the congregation. People are less likely to burn out, and their gifts and time are treated more respectfully. The paid staff members equip individuals for participation in ministry instead of serving as sole providers of all services pertaining to church life. The congregation recognizes and affirms the ministry of its members that also goes on beyond the walls of the church—within their own families, neighborhoods, workplaces, schools, and communities. In short, shared ministry has the potential to turn a congregation around. A faith community concentrating on building a culture that pays great attention to the gifts of all its members—that nurtures their growth and development and supports them in a systematic way—will find itself attracting more members and carrying out its unique mission more effectively than previously imagined possible. Let's look at some scenarios in which shared ministry can help solve a problem.

LOSS OF MEMBERSHIP

Congregations that have lost a large part of their membership through the aging and death of many of their members, changed demographics, and various internal problems often look at the future bleakly. Denominational leaders and pastors may assume these congregations will continue to spiral downward and that the job of their leaders is to preside over an orderly, pastorally sensitive, slow but inevitable demise. In some cases, this may be a realistic appraisal. But in others the potential exists for this struggling faith community to rediscover its historical roots—the vision founding members had for the congregation. The faith community can reclaim its original energy and regain passion for the mission it now sees for itself. To accomplish this requires that the leadership delve into the history of the parish and note what gifts those early members brought to the life of the community. Similarly, the parish needs to make a concentrated effort to discover and nurture the gifts of its members, to research the needs of the surrounding community, and to draw out the potential hidden in the people yet to be invited to participate. By reworking its purpose to reflect these changing realities, a congregation can restore itself to growth and new life. A shared ministry system can be of great help in accomplishing these tasks.

STUCK ON A PLATEAU

Some congregations can reach plateaus on which they linger and then begin a downward slide, with loss of members and burnout among those left behind. A shared ministry system will encourage such a parish to revisit its purpose, expectations, and ways of doing things. In reimagining itself through this process, a congregation can find new meaning, direction, and energy to revitalize its identity. The shared ministry structure is of great help in determining what components of effective volunteer ministry need to be reassessed.

GROWING PAINS

A congregation may experience growing pains. As more and more people come to such a church, it struggles to keep up under trying circumstances, such as inadequate staff numbers, cramped physical space, and ineffective ways of doing things. In this situation shared ministry offers a way to cope with these challenges by establishing new ways to invite members into ministry, designing creative processes to organize and support them, and adapting the role of paid staff to equip more and more members for participating in the church's work. The fact that the congregation is experiencing difficulty can open its leaders and staff up to a new way of approaching congregational life: shared ministry.

LOSS OF A KEY LEADER

One might assume congregations that seem successful by most measures have no need to change the way they do things. But I have observed that even these faith communities can face challenges. Perhaps a dynamic founding pastor or key staff person leaves. A pastor who was a charismatic person with visionary leadership or one who liked to tightly control every aspect of the congregation's ministry may have made people too dependent on the pastor's decisions. Consequently a leadership vacuum occurs when this person leaves. A new pastor may experience difficult challenges in encouraging more active participation from lay members. Building a system of shared ministry will help to bring about this increased involvement by parishioners.

ENTRENCHED LAY LEADERS

Sometimes lay leaders may be so competent and stay in their positions for such a long time that it is difficult to bring along potential new members to grow into the leadership roles. Issues of who "owns" the ministry of the faith community can arise. It may be impossible for new leaders to follow in the footsteps of these longtime superheroes. This situation may also mean that nothing is in place for bringing new members into ministry and making them feel not only welcomed but also important contributors to the community. Shared ministry can help to change this culture into a sharing one.

COMPLACENCY

Getting too comfortable with the status quo may cause congregation leaders to fail to notice and prepare for changing needs in membership or for evolving community circumstances. Over time the dedicated early founders and original creators of ministries age out or may burn out. The ethnic makeup of a community may change. Failure to constantly assess leadership turnover and to plan for future eventualities may cause volunteer ministry to shrink alarmingly. Shared ministry promotes a system where no one person or group owns a ministry; instead, the entire congregation owns *all* the ministries collectively. A plan is in place for creating feeder systems to provide new leaders as the need arises.

DROP IN FINANCIAL GIVING

Frequently a congregation will experience both a lack of volunteer ministers and a drop in financial contributions at the same time. The two aspects usually do go hand in hand. Another key benefit of shared ministry, well known in the nonprofit world and equally applicable to congregations, is that the more people are involved in volunteer work in the organization, the more financial contributions increase. People who feel a strong connection to the work of their faith community, who experience partnerships with staff members, and who are encouraged to play significant roles in the planning and decision-making process will often increase their financial support as well. Their sense of belonging and feeling valued prompt them to contribute both time and money to the success of the community.

FIXATION ON HOSPITALITY

One faith community with which I worked identified its waning participation in ministry as a hospitality issue. Members thought that if they somehow could get people to become more hospitable to newcomers, the number of ministry volunteers would increase. While it is true that hospitality is an important issue in many churches, hospitality alone will not necessarily achieve ministry participation. The shared ministry system enables a congregation to build processes that not only welcome new members but also help people identify their gifts and how they can best use them in the church. Shared ministry deepens and extends the hospitality theme by helping newer members become involved in small ministry groups in which they can begin to develop relationships as they contribute their gifts to the work of a ministry and thereby feel more a part of congregational life.

BUILDING A NEW CONGREGATION

A congregation just beginning its life has a wonderful opportunity to build in this comprehensive system right from the beginning. Building a culture from the ground up is always easier than changing an existing one.

Shared ministry presents a proven method of gathering the gifts of all members, building ways to design ministries, creating new ministries, and supporting existing ones. It helps the faith community to find creative ways to recruit ministry leaders and members, paying attention to present-day needs of volunteer ministers. In such a congregation, leaders place emphasis on inviting people to participate in ministries that match their interests, gifts, and available time. Staff and lay leaders are open to new ways of doing things, to new ideas, and particularly to establishing a true collaborative relationship between paid staff and ministry volunteers. The pastor encourages the staff to empower members and equip them to perform their ministries. Shared ministry offers a blueprint to reach these goals. It fosters mutual respect and sharing in the work of the church, according to God's direction.

Why Shared Ministry Works

Shared ministry succeeds where other efforts fail because it builds a foundation and culture that stays in place throughout the life of the congregation. If woven deeply enough and strongly enough into the warp and woof of congregational life, shared ministry will sustain itself through leadership transitions as well as other challenges. The faith community's culture carries a momentum of its own by continually inviting in new people and supporting its members in their ministries. This system regularly involves congregation members in evaluating all the processes of engaging members in the church's ministry. Because all shared ministry components are performed by members themselves, in partnership with paid staff members and ordained clergy, the components remain operational within the congregation despite any changes in leadership.

In addition, if the congregation chooses to participate in some particular new strategic planning method, to create a new mission or vision statement, or to start a new initiative, shared ministry offers an established network of relationships, support, and collaboration on which new efforts can be built.

Shared ministry is a comprehensive system that creates satisfying and effective ministry. Many congregations have some components of shared ministry well in hand. Or particular ministry areas or individual ministries may have many of the components in place and working well. However, it is rare to see a church that has a consistent, across-the-board, multifaceted system covering all ministries. When there is no uniformity, individuals working within various ministries may have completely different volunteer experiences, depending on how much of the system each ministry has developed. Some members may be quickly invited into ministry, warmly welcomed, and suitably prepared to participate in the volunteer group. Others may never be contacted after volunteering their gifts or may experience poor orientation to their positions and a lack of support. This uneven experience of working in ministry causes many people to feel unsure about continuing, because they don't know what to expect from one ministry to the next or from one leader to the next. The comprehensive approach that shared ministry offers ensures that all members involved in ministry will have similar experiences as they participate in their service. It also ensures that no essential aspect of volunteer service will be overlooked in any given ministry. Individuals will be invited to serve in a ministry that can make good use of their gifts. Their time will not be wasted. No offer to share gifts will be ignored.

Shared ministry not only assists in calling people into ministry but also keeps them there; it does so by placing them in positions in which they can use their gifts, building in good training processes, supporting them in their work, helping to create reasonable expectations regarding the amount of work required in each position, and meeting their needs for scheduling and their available time.

Shared ministry advocates many processes that are designed to prevent burnout. These include asking volunteers to make a yearly recommitment to their ministry, thereby providing a graceful way to opt out of a particular ministry or try a new one. Longtime ministry members are encouraged to share the ministry with new people as well as delegate to and refrain from micromanaging other ministry members. Congregations with a solid shared ministry system also give permission to people to say no when approached with a request for help, without being made to feel guilty.

Ultimately, shared ministry benefits congregations because the number of people involved in ministry grows. Energy and commitment remain high, and fewer capable people are lost just because they have been doing too much for too long. For all these reasons, shared ministry offers an excellent way to create ownership in the life of the parish by the members. It increases participation in the mission of the faith community in a coherent, planned, and effective manner. It grows the church and provides a model for achieving a contributing and engaged membership.

CHAPTER 3

Working with Staff

S hared ministry is not just one more program of the church that can operate independently. Creating a shared ministry culture and building the system that brings it about will affect virtually every aspect of a congregation's life. The shared ministry director will work directly with the pastor and paid staff to grow the ministry of the congregation. Every component of shared ministry—designing ministries, recruitment, support, gifts discovery, data management, and so forth—will increase the number of members involved in ministry and enrich the ministry experience of each participant. But close cooperation with paid staff is required to make that a reality. For example, a comprehensive recruitment campaign depends on staff providing information about ministries for the recruitment booklet, ministry leaders helping to prepare position descriptions, the pastor and other worship leaders planning and leading a meaningful worship experience centered on a theme, and staff and lay leaders promptly following up after the recruitment event. When the shared ministry director and team, pastor, and paid staff cooperate and communicate well, congregations can expect a successful outcome to the event and to the development of a shared ministry culture.

Four Premises

In a survey given to experienced directors of shared ministry, a recurring theme in their responses was that taking the time to establish relationships with the executive pastor and paid staff was important to their success. My own experience working with staff and pastors bears this out. Time spent here will pay big dividends down the road as you lay the groundwork for understanding, co-operation, collaboration, and support with all staff members.

Here are the basic premises from which to operate:

1. The extent to which shared ministry becomes a thriving part of your church culture will depend in large part on how it is received, adopted, and incorporated by staff into their practice as they work with members of the congregation.
2. Plan on splitting your time about fifty-fifty between building specific components of the shared ministry system and working with individual staff members and lay leaders to persuade, educate, and train them in the elements you are building, model it for them, as well as support their efforts to develop a shared ministry system.
3. This process takes a very long time.
4. It is worth it!

Let's examine these premises in more depth. You may find the first premise counterintuitive, because shared ministry is about working with volunteers. But even if a majority of your members are in full accord with the principles and structures of shared ministry, if the paid staff and member leaders are not behind it, it won't happen in your church. Here's why I say that. Unless you are working in a small congregation—less than one hundred members—you are not going to be able to interface with each and every member on a regular basis. Instead, you will need to rely on the other paid staff and unpaid lay leaders to do that connecting. If these frontline individuals don't have a thorough understanding of what a shared ministry culture looks like at the ministry level and are not convinced that building the culture is worth the effort, they will not be able to create it. In fact, you may discover that staff members are working at cross-purposes with you in making needed changes.

Because staff support is so important, this brings us to the second premise: it will be critical to the success of shared ministry in your congregation to spend time with staff educating them and motivating them to work with you within their own ministry arenas. Members of the church will experience the tenets of shared ministry primarily through their interactions with the paid staff. Therefore, if the pastor and paid staff are not fully informed about and on board with the concept of shared ministry, they will likely behave in ways that, unwittingly or not, put roadblocks on the path toward your vision. To lessen the chances of this happening, you will have to split your time equally between your role as system designer and your role as relationship builder with the staff. Every component of building a shared ministry culture requires the participation and support of the rest of the congregation's leaders. Even an attitude of indifference will interfere with key processes, such as writing position descriptions, following up on recruitment lists, planning and hosting appreciation and celebration events, and following risk management screening procedures, to name a few.

Third, you must have a vision of a process that takes years to complete, and you must be committed to working on that process for the long run, for five to ten years and beyond. Remember that shared ministry is not a program. It is a system, a belief structure, and a culture. It demands consistent and committed attention. Systems and cultures are not created in the space of one short program year. They gradually develop over a significant amount of time. In addition, if you approach your plans, hopes, and dreams with this long-run thinking, you will be more apt to relax about minor setbacks or perceived failures along the way. So will your pastor and staff. This is also why the shared ministry committee is so important. Regardless of changes in staff as time goes by, the committee needs to carry the concept of shared ministry from year to year and even from pastor to pastor. The shared ministry committee members are the true stewards of the culture.

Fourth, what you achieve by working through all these challenges is worth the effort. Starting your work with a one- to two-year plan will give you perspective and a big picture foundation from which to assess initial progress. Revisiting the plan at least annually and adding new goals and steps to achieving them will keep you on track as well as help you see the progress you are making. You will have a leading part in creating a new, vibrant, committed body of believers. People will serve in the various ministries of the congregation by using their special gifts, passions, experience, and available time. Every person who wishes to get involved in a ministry will receive a follow-up contact. Each person will be assisted in finding the right fit for his or her unique needs. Burnout will significantly decrease, because people are working in ministries that match their gifts and interests.

The ministries themselves will be designed with today's busy members in mind. Position descriptions will help each person determine whether they have the time, skills, and desire required for a particular ministry position. No ministry will necessarily last forever; those that are no longer needed will be let go. No member will be expected to commit his or her entire life to a specific ministry. Your members will be able to gracefully leave a ministry and move on to others. Ministries will thrive and make significant contributions to the mission of the church. People will serve willingly and happily. Staff will act as equippers for ministry, supporting, training, and mentoring ministry members to perform the work of the ministry. Your faith community will come alive with newfound energy.

To have a role to play in creating such a community is one of the most satisfying experiences a person can have. If you have the opportunity to work long enough to build a deep and broad culture, you will see the fruits of your labors for years to come.

Congregations without a paid director, that rely on a volunteer director or shared ministry committee, will have to deal with different issues. Volunteer directors and committees will generally have less influence with other paid staff than another paid staff member will have. Building credibility and gaining access to staff will be two challenges for volunteers. Keeping communication lines open and getting staff support for projects are other challenges. It is wise for the congregation to select excellent leaders for the committee, people who are capable of grasping the intricacies of their position, and to provide the committee with a very supportive staff liaison. Nevertheless, the shared ministry committee should not rely solely on their staff liaison for communication with the other paid staff of the congregation. The committee needs to pay attention to building their own relationships with the pastor and paid staff.

Key Leadership Roles and Relationships

The pastor is the key leader in obtaining cooperation and participation from all the other staff and unpaid lay leaders. The pastor must be passionately committed to the vision of gifted people working in full partnership with staff facilitators to bring about the realm of God. However, the parish and staff will take their cues from the pastor. If she is not committed to the vision, she will exhibit certain cues—subtle or not so subtle—that your congregation and staff members will pick up on. For example, the pastor might say, "This sounds good, and I really like what has been presented, but we (I) have more important programs and concerns right now." Or, "I question whether our parishioners have the _____ (you fill in the blank: ability, knowledge, gifts, sense of responsibility, or right) to act in full partnership with us." Or, "You have my full support in this. Go ahead and make it happen. That is what we hired you for. I leave it all in your hands."

Other behavioral cues can include such things as consistently keeping volunteer leaders out of the main decision-making or problem-solving processes related to their areas of giftedness and responsibility, micromanaging staff or lay volunteer leaders, or quickly blaming them for every mistake, glitch, or issue that arises. Some cues may be subtler. But upon reflection they may indicate what the real issue most likely is. For example, the pastor might show indirectly by his actions and decisions, but not in so many words, "This is all about power, and I'm not giving up any of mine. Thanks anyway," or "I'm not willing to designate significant amounts of money, time, or staff positions to this endeavor."

While a pastor may not say exactly these words, if you hear similar ideas or consistent themes or reactions, it is a good bet that your pastor lacks understanding or simply doesn't want to support the initiative. Other telltale signals are the pastor undermining the plan or your leadership by countermanding agreed-upon decisions and procedures, failing to include you in leadership meetings and issues, or failing to treat you as an equal partner and member of the staff. Because the shared ministry director position is often a new one for the congregation, and may be new for the individual hired for the position, that person may not even realize that he is being sidelined and given little meaningful support. This is more likely to happen when the director is unfamiliar with the cultural milieu the staff and pastor are used to working in. He may not realize that he should be part of staff leadership meetings and decisions. He may assume that it is normal for the pastor to second-guess every action of each staff person. After all, she is the pastor and the shared ministry director's "boss." A helpful guiding principle in these matters is to compare the resources, respect, and support given to a director of religious education to the resources, respect, and support given to you. The two should be on a par with each other.

ASSESSING PASTOR ATTITUDES

Following is a set of questions that can be used in a couple of ways. Depending on the nature of the relationship between the shared ministry director and the pastor, you might have a candid discussion with the pastor centered on these statements. Or you might suggest that the pastor take the list of questions and think about how she would answer them. The questions bring to the foreground many of the issues that affect the level of support you are likely to receive from the pastor. Another way to use them is to answer them as you believe the pastor is likely to. This works particularly well if you know the individual and have worked with her for a while. Putting yourself into the mindset of the pastor will give you some indications of how supportive she will be.

- Am I fully committed to releasing the gifts of God's people for mission in the world, even if that means I will be stretched in the process?
- Am I willing to commit resources of time, money, and staff, as well as my personal support, to enable this to happen?
- Do I have the ability to work collaboratively with others? If not, am I willing to learn how to do this? Can I share power without feeling threatened? Am I willing to share appropriate parts of my ministerial role with others?
- Am I open to change, even change in my own thinking and ways of doing things, to bring about growth and spiritual maturity for the members of this congregation?
- Do I trust God to direct and lead our congregation to a fuller realization of God's plan for us by trusting and empowering God's people?

The pastor must present the vision for shared ministry and make it clear that all staff and lay leaders are expected to work toward it. The pastor's support has to be 100 percent. The pastor and director of shared ministry must have a close working relationship; they must be partners in their common goal to bring the people's best gifts to God's work.

THE SHARED MINISTRY DIRECTOR'S ROLE

The shared ministry director must be seen by the staff as another holder of the vision, a resource and expert to go to with questions and problems relating to lay volunteer ministry. This person must be seen as a fair, honest companion worker in the church world. She or he must be able to identify and work within clear boundaries of professionalism, confidentiality, and trust. Turf protection, politicking, power struggles, and us-versus-them mentalities will spell the death of the shared ministry dream. The shared ministry director must take no part in these destructive actions.

The director of shared ministry must be fully committed to the ideal as well. She or he must have time to work on the project. In my experience, it doesn't work for shared ministry to be just one of the many hats worn by a staff member who has other responsibilities. Inevitably, the other responsibilities will take precedence.

Consider a staff member who is director of shared ministry as well as director of religious education and a pastoral caregiver for a congregation. Similar combinations of job responsibilities are common in a lot of congregations. When one hundred grade school children and ten volunteer teachers are going to arrive at 4:00 p.m. for their religious education classes, the staff person is going to spend her day preparing for those classes. She is not going to put that task on hold to plan a shared ministry commissioning ceremony two months from now. Then on a day when no religious education classes are scheduled and the staff person plans to have the time, suddenly, a pastoral care emergency occurs, and because she's wearing that hat too, the emergency takes precedence. On it goes.

Building a system, a parish culture, takes the full attention and time (depending on the size of the congregation) of a staff person to create the components, to build relationships with staff and congregation members, and to handle hundreds of details that surround such a system. It can't be at the bottom of somebody's priority list and survive in the busy world of church life. In smaller congregations, someone working part time or as a volunteer director can move the system building along, though not as fast as a full-time director, of course.

Most important is that the director—whether full time or part time—not be responsible for several jobs simultaneously. Some congregations choose to start out with a paid staff member handling the shared ministry responsibility in addition to other roles. While this appears to work for a short time, in my experience, it ultimately leads to dissatisfaction by all concerned. The staff person feels overburdened with too many competing responsibilities. He may experience guilt at seldom having the time to attend to the shared ministry part of his position. The staff member may suffer serious burnout as he struggles to keep up with too many demands.

Pastors and lay leaders may also experience frustration as they perceive that the congregation is not moving ahead in any meaningful way in changing its culture. They may become disillusioned with progress that is much slower than expected. In this situation there is a tendency to mistakenly assume the failure is due to the concept of shared ministry or of the shared ministry team or director. "We tried that and it doesn't work." The statement reveals a lack of understanding that changing a culture requires consistent effort, a lot of hard work, and lots of time. The director of shared ministry has a large responsibility to raise awareness of these facts among staff and members and to set realistic expectations for the staff members and congregation at large.

If faith communities discover the director isn't able to fulfill their expectations for the ministry, they can change their strategy. Some congregations that initially expect one person to manage multiple responsibilities, including shared ministry, eventually realize that the director of shared ministry is too bogged down in the demands of numerous roles, and so they gradually increase the paid staff member's hours assigned for shared ministry work. Another tactic some churches use is to realign staff responsibilities to free up the shared ministry director to concentrate on that responsibility alone.

Another issue in some congregations is determining who should supervise the director of shared ministry. In almost all cases, the pastor is the appropriate supervisor for this position. For best results there needs to be a direct relationship between the two positions. The director of shared ministry is a leadership position, not an administrative one, though it has administrative components. In my experience, it rarely works to put business administrators or similar people in supervisory positions over shared ministry directors. I have the utmost respect for business administrators, but I think if you look carefully at the gifts and emphases for these two types of positions, you will find that they are necessarily very different. In larger congregations, a business administrator is mainly concerned with handling the financial resources of the parish, keeping the physical plant in good shape, attending to budgets and accounting processes, overseeing healthy business practices and the congregation's organization in these areas, and supervising support staff. In smaller congregations, additional responsibilities may include handling everything from scheduling meeting space to keeping track of the personal records of members, to managing the computers and phone systems, to updating the website. The business administrator usually brings gifts of attention to detail, familiarity with financial processes and planning, good project management skills, and the like. The focus for a shared ministry director, on the other hand, is establishing relationships with people, building systemic processes for managing culture change, evaluating the progress of the congregation toward the major goals, and incorporating more members into the ministry of that congregation. Some of the gifts a director of shared ministry brings to the faith community are vision, people skills, and the ability to work with multiple details while keeping the big picture clearly in focus. Major frustration will likely occur when you put an administrator in charge of the director of shared ministry.

There is a second problem with having a business administrator supervising a director of shared ministry. Such an arrangement effectively insulates the pastor from knowledge of and involvement with the director of shared ministry. The pastor will get his information about progress, issues, and struggles secondhand, through the reports of the supervisor. It will be more difficult for the director of shared ministry to communicate directly with the pastor and share parts of the vision with him on an ongoing and fairly informal basis. Inserting another staff person between the pastor and the director of shared ministry makes it likely that the pastor will be less involved and committed to advancing the vision, because he will not be paying direct attention to it for significant periods.

Shared ministry is different from other areas and positions in a congregation. It affects virtually every member on some level. The focus for shared ministry is on the ministerial health of the entire faith community. It is not limited to only education or worship or the pastoral care of individuals. Shared ministry influences the direction the congregation is heading in a holistic sense. This has everything to do with setting a vision for how ministry occurs throughout the entire community and moving that community toward realizing that vision. This spells leadership in every sense. The pastor, the recognized leader of a congregation, must be in close contact with the shared ministry director to assure the vision is mutually understood between them, to provide support to each other in advancing the shared ministry initiative, and to join forces in achieving shared goals.

However, depending on the gifts and focus of the individual business administrator, working in a collegial relationship with a knowledgeable, supportive person can be of tremendous benefit to both parties. But this requires a business administrator who possesses and values people skills and believes building relationships is as important as financial concerns. With the pastor as the supervisor of the director of shared ministry, both the business administrator and the shared ministry director can work in their respective areas of giftedness without the stress of the business administrator needing to supervise a leadership position whose major function is relationship building and culture change.

WAYS TO DEVELOP RELATIONSHIPS WITH STAFF

So exactly how can the director of shared ministry build these important relationships? Here are some examples that may be helpful.

- Starting from the point when the director of shared ministry is hired or appointed, the pastor, paid staff, and director may participate in an initial meeting, possibly facilitated by an outside consultant. The goal of such a session would be to come to a mutual understanding about questions such as, What are our staff expectations of the job of director of shared ministry? What are the pastor's expectations? What are the new director's expectations? What kind of support will the director of shared ministry need? This conversation puts everyone on the same page from the beginning.
- The director of shared ministry can arrange for personal interviews with each staff person, getting to know them as individuals. What do they do? What are their gifts? What are their challenges and problems working with volunteer ministers?
- The director of shared ministry can look for opportunities to collaborate with other staff on joint projects. This shows that she or he is a team player who also has valuable gifts and insight to bring to the situation. Affirmation and support for the other staff in their roles—for example, working on staff appreciation events as hard as the shared ministry director works on volunteer appreciation—is a necessity.
- The director of shared ministry should refer gifted new members and others who are interested in a particular ministry to appropriate staff. Nothing makes friends more quickly than providing capable, gifted volunteer ministers to overworked staff.
- The director of shared ministry should act as a resource for groups and staff with recruiting needs. This does not mean the shared ministry director assumes responsibility for doing

the recruiting. It means she offers lists of potential volunteer workers from the shared ministry database, suggests effective advertising methods, teaches invitational methods of getting people involved, and so forth.

- The director of shared ministry assists paid staff and volunteer coordinators in creating position descriptions for the volunteer ministries they work with.
- The director of shared ministry can counsel individual staff members on problems working with volunteer ministers.
- The director of shared ministry should present staff development workshops that address areas of concern and that illustrate the principles of shared ministry and contribute to staff growth. Examples might include training in how to do recruitment year-round or how to supervise volunteers effectively or exploring leadership styles.
- It is essential that the director of shared ministry always follow up on every request and suggestion that comes to him from parishioners, whether this means delegating it or personally looking into the situation and then getting back to the individual with an answer, no matter what.

The better the staff understands what the role of the shared ministry director is supposed to be and how the director can and will assist them with the volunteers they work with in ministry, the less likely it is that he or she will encounter misunderstandings, work at cross-purposes, or encounter barriers to changing the culture of the congregation.

BUILDING RELATIONSHIPS WITH MEMBERS

Establishing strong relationships with congregation members is a separate but still important aspect of the shared ministry director's work. Members of the congregation include those in leadership positions, such as boards, members and committees chairs, the

active laity in all the ministries, and the general parish membership. The director of shared ministry must be seen as a fair, honest,
reliable, and passionate advocate for the vision of shared ministry.

It is also essential that the director of shared ministry create
and work with a shared ministry volunteer team for support, feedback, planning, assistance, and reality checks regarding the major
components of the system as they are worked on. Building relationships with members is an essential part of the overall system
the shared ministry director tends to in a congregation. Without
such relationships, success in creating a shared ministry culture
will be difficult to achieve.

CHAPTER 4

Creating a Base of Support

P reparation is absolutely the key to accomplishing a cultural change in any organization. Nowhere is this truer than in a church setting. Corporations may dictate a change in direction for their organization to which all employees are obligated to adhere. However, mandates are usually unsuccessful in achieving lasting change in organizations where participation is optional. Culture change in a congregation depends on the goodwill and desire of members to initiate the change and on their cooperation in the hard work of accomplishing it.

Nothing will set you up for disappointing results, if not outright failure, more than charging ahead without laying the groundwork first. This culture shift requires that all leaders understand and participate willingly in the change. There are many layers of leaders, from staff to volunteer. Each person at every level has an influence on if and how the change is instituted in his or her own area. Changes need to occur throughout the parish structure and depend on the participation of a majority of members. This can be achieved only by providing time for people to prepare, discuss, and explore how the changes can be brought about and what they will look like in any given ministry area, as well as why it is important to make the changes in the first place.

In an informal survey I conducted with a group of directors of volunteer ministries about helping a congregation adopt a shared ministry culture, several themes emerged. I asked directors two questions:

- Looking back, what was the most helpful piece of information or advice you received when you began your job?
- What is one thing you wish you had done, known, or planned for when you started your job?

I heard essentially the same response to both of these questions. Some said they were advised to seek senior pastor, staff, and lay leadership buy-in at the very beginning. Those who did this found it much easier to proceed and obtain the support necessary to implement change. On the flip side, respondents who struggled reported that they wished they had done this when they assumed their position.

Those who had struggled had plunged ahead with building the components, getting just so far into the process, only to discover that they needed to go back and achieve that understanding and buy-in from the paid staff, pastor, and congregation leaders. This in turn slowed or even halted progress until they were able to achieve support from a broadened base.

So what do you do? Where do you start?

The first step is to recruit the shared ministry director and team.

- Option 1: Recruit the core team first, allowing time for their formation, and then recruit either a paid or a nonpaid director of shared ministry.
- Option 2: Hire a director of shared ministry at the outset and encourage that person to recruit his or her own team with whom to work.

Recruiting a Team First

Some congregations have already identified a need to "do something about volunteers." In this case, it may be fairly easy to recruit members for a team or committee interested in learning more about the value of a shared ministry system and willing to help bring it about. This committee will learn about the system and then teach others about it, providing the support and leadership to begin building the culture, piece by piece. The shared ministry team can advocate adding the position of director of shared ministry as a staff position. They can compose a rationale identifying benefits for initiating such a position and bring this proposal to the governing board. Representatives from this group can also be part of the search group for a good candidate. Finally, they can assist the newly appointed shared ministry director with planning, visioning, and staying grounded in the realities of congregational life.

In some small parishes congregation leaders and the shared ministry committee can do this learning piece together. This is possible because they typically have fewer people in leadership positions, and responsibilities are shared more informally. In addition, there is often a custom for frequent meetings that include both paid staff and key volunteer ministers. So adding an educational component to these meetings that includes all these leaders is easier to do.

In medium to larger churches, it seems to work better to commission the team to do their study first and then present their ideas and recommendations to the staff and lay leaders. There are several reasons for this. First, the number of leaders is much higher. Also, paid staff members are more likely to have responsibilities to attend numerous meetings already, so it may be difficult for them to commit to putting yet another meeting on their calendars. Large churches may not have a precedent for all paid staff and lay leaders to meet together on an ongoing basis. It may be more efficient to offer a leadership workshop or retreat day that can be designed to present the big picture to the congregation's paid and unpaid leaders.

TIPS FOR RECRUITING A TEAM

Good candidates for this team are people who have a broad understanding of the needs of the church as a whole. Effective team members usually have the following types of experience:

- Serving as a member on the congregation's board
- Working with and as a volunteer
- Working in professional human resource management
- Involving people in the church's ministries and mission
- Exercising gifts of hospitality and welcoming
- Researching or building databases
- Building systems, understanding their importance, how they function, how to create and improve them
- Speaking in public
- Employing a wide variety of communication tools
- Planning major initiatives, including both the big picture and the details

Sometimes the pastor or board may appoint current board members who are strongly invested in the current culture and seem unable to think creatively. They may be burned out from all the board duties already required of them. In this case, starting out with a slate of committee members that includes people newer to the congregation can help move the congregation forward to a new vision and mission.

It is important that the pastor be an ex-officio member of the team or committee and that he or she attend meetings regularly for at least the first year. A staff liaison and a representative from the governing board are other important people to have at the planning meetings. These three people need not take on the actual work of the shared ministry team, but they need to be in on the ground floor, learning about the system, observing the discussions and decision-making processes of the team, supporting the group and its efforts, and generally becoming knowledgeable about shared ministry. Participation in these planning meetings will allow them to present concepts, needs, and recommendations to other important groups in the faith community. They can act as strong advocates and supporters of this new initiative.

An effective team generally includes five to seven people. If the committee gets too large, members can have difficulty achieving consensus in a reasonable amount of time. Members might also sit on the sidelines, not taking their position seriously enough to pull their weight on the team. On the other hand, it is important for the committee to be large enough to represent the major segments of the congregation's membership. A committee that is too small can lack the breadth of experience and variety of attitudes, ideas, and gifts that will enable it to lead the congregation to this new vision of a faith community.

ADVANTAGES AND DISADVANTAGES

This option has several advantages. Creating a core team builds a strong base of understanding and support from within the faith community from the outset. Lacking a staff member position in shared ministry, team members will be more likely to educate themselves in the principles of shared ministry, instead of depending on a staff person to direct them. Key staff members, especially the pastor, are also more likely to meet with the core team and learn about the system from the outset. Pastors usually want to be closely involved with any group that is doing this kind of big-picture planning, especially if no other staff member is available to work with the group. The pastor's involvement immediately brings a stamp of approval and signifies the importance of this new team and its work. To encourage the pastor to participate in planning, the team may need to explain to him or her that it will be dealing with measures that will affect the entire congregation. The shared ministry team is not just another ministry planning its programs.

Sometimes another advantage to this option is that the learning proceeds more rapidly. Some faith communities are able to identify a potential director of volunteer ministries from within their membership. Often this person is already a member of the shared ministry committee. As time goes on it becomes apparent that this individual would be perfect in the position. By group consensus and the invitation of the pastor or board, the individual is asked to accept leadership of the shared ministry initiative. Because the potential paid staff member has been part of the initial learning and decision-making processes from the beginning, progress is made much more quickly than would be the case if an individual were hired from outside the congregation, after the shared ministry committee had already been formed.

A disadvantage to this strategy is that the shared ministry system will necessarily grow more slowly without someone concentrating full time on building the components. Even the most dedicated team of volunteers will not be able to affect the system, nor influence other staff members, as effectively or quickly as a qualified paid director of shared ministry. One director told me she needed to be in front of staff every day, modeling and promoting the principles of shared ministry in all that was happening in the parish.

A second disadvantage is that once the shared ministry director is finally put into place, he or she will need to be oriented to what has been learned and accomplished, the priorities identified, and plans that have been made. This will slow down the process until the director gets up to speed.

Another disadvantage can be that team members may not be willing to turn over responsibilities to the new staff person or may become impatient when the staff person needs to take time to learn about the culture and needs of the community before moving ahead.

Recruiting a Director First

A new director of shared ministry can be hired first. The new director of shared ministry then collaborates with the pastor and several other leaders to identify talent for the committee. Arguments can be made on both sides of the question of whether to hire from within the congregation or bring in someone from the outside. I discussed above the scenario where a committee member is hired to take the director position.

In addition to speeding up the director's learning about shared ministry, hiring from within the congregation brings benefits in that the individual is already familiar with the current culture, knows more members, and understands the organizational structure of the faith community. One disadvantage reported by directors hired from within the congregation is that they can never be off duty, because they worship where they work and are known to many. There is also the challenge of maintaining boundaries between one's professional position and one's friendships with other members of the faith community. Hiring from outside the congregation eliminates many boundary issues. Because this person has no prior experience with the congregation, she brings a new perspective and fresh ideas to the position. Her newness allows her to ask questions and make observations that a congregation member may not be comfortable doing.

Many congregations, claiming financial difficulties, prefer initially to appoint an unpaid director of volunteer ministry. Another common practice is making the position part time. Because this position is unfamiliar to many leaders and not well understood, even if they have heard of it, many prefer to test out the position before supporting it fully. What inevitably happens is that the unpaid volunteer director who starts out working part time soon finds himself pressured to do more as the system begins to take hold and the magnitude of the work necessary to keep it growing becomes more apparent. Then either the system ceases to develop because the volunteer cannot contribute any more time or the leaders come to realize the value of the position and authorize changing it to a paid position, which gradually increases from a part-time to a full-time one. From my observations of congregations that create a director of shared ministry position, it doesn't take long for them to realize that this is a key leadership role that ultimately needs to be fully funded.

ROLE OF THE TEAM

Even with an active paid staff person in place, a shared ministry team is a necessary part of the process. A clear statement of the roles and expectations for the team and the director need to be settled on, however. Typically, the team assists with planning, offering the benefit of their familiarity with the community, their creativity, and their energy for the work. The team also assists with planning and executing certain key events in the shared ministry cycle, such as preparing for the annual recruitment drive, spearheading ministry appreciation events, welcoming congregation members, and providing hospitality to large shared ministry events throughout the year. The team keeps the director of shared ministry grounded in the reality of congregation life. The team can challenge a director to enlarge an idea or point out when an idea is not practical. The volunteer shared ministry team has its fingers on the pulse of the faith community, which is an invaluable asset for the director. Without that support, the director sometimes operates in a vacuum.

Because no one may fully understand or appreciate what the shared ministry director is doing or why he is doing it, congregations may be tempted during economic downturns to eliminate the position if no one other than the individual currently in the position advocates keeping it. The shared ministry director is in a unique position. A lot of the work goes on behind the scenes. A board that is unfamiliar with the director's work can easily assume that because they haven't seen him doing much, the position is probably expendable. A wise director will cultivate relationships with board members, key staff people, and the pastor as well as the shared ministry committee. Frequent communication explaining what is happening behind the scenes, his role in making it happen, and the impact that the work has had or is having will help keep the importance of the position clearly in front of the leaders. To accomplish this without appearing too self-important, the director can use the word *we* in describing actions with which the director had assistance. Other ways to gain support include accenting the impact of the action being described and pointing out how specific tasks were accomplished because of this unique position. For example, "We (or the committee and I) spent a lot of time strategizing how best to present the need for position descriptions for every ministry." "I was able to do quite a bit of research to discover the best software available to use in tracking volunteer minister participation. Because I was able to spend this time, we will be able to move ahead much more swiftly in getting the software I am recommending up and running."

The shared ministry team members are partners with the director in promoting the new culture. Through their contacts and positions, they can advocate new processes at a grassroots level and explain why they are important. They can also be active cheerleaders for the position of director of shared ministry.

The qualities to look for in a potential director of shared ministry include the following:

- System builder, synthesizer, connector
- Able to see the big picture, a visioner
- Skilled in dealing with details, details, details
- Very organized
- A leader and a team player
- Collaborative, a sharer of power
- Excellent trainer
- Excellent communicator
- Focused, yet able to multitask
- Committed to follow-up
- Skilled at delegating
- Enjoys seeing people excel
- Lifelong learner, totally authentic person

ADVANTAGES AND DISADVANTAGES

An advantage to first recruiting the director of shared ministry is that the director and the team can work and learn together almost from the beginning. The director will likely obtain support from a team that she has handpicked.

Another major advantage is that a director is usually able to create more momentum, which is difficult to achieve when a group meets only every few weeks or even monthly, so the start-up will go more quickly. A director might more easily communicate with other staff and key leaders, because they have more frequent opportunities to connect, so shared ministry will be better integrated into, and will more significantly influence, other work of the congregation. Also, no matter how good working relationships are between paid staff members and volunteer ministers, a paid staff member will usually have more credibility and influence among other staff, who will pay more attention to her ideas than to someone who is not a staff member.

Disadvantages can include the difficulty a new staff member in the church may have in identifying appropriate people to serve on the shared ministry committee. She may have an inclination to try to work alone at the beginning, thus distancing herself and the process from the heart of the parish during those important beginning steps. Efforts to collaborate may be put on hold while the new director of shared ministry attempts to get a handle on her job, the culture of the congregation, how things work, and so forth.

Beginning Tasks

The shared ministry team, or the new staff person working in conjunction with the team, should create a mission statement that expresses the role they see for themselves. An example is "Mission of the Shared Ministry Team: to promote a system that invites, encourages, and supports the gifts and participation of each member in the mission of Faith and Hope Congregation." Without a mission statement to guide the work of the shared ministry team and staff person, it is easy to get so busy with details that the sense of purpose in fulfilling the congregation's mission and the mission itself can be lost. Losing sight of the mission can prevent the team and staff person from setting priorities wisely and making plans that will be effective in moving the mission forward.

Obtaining early buy-in from staff, governing and advising boards, the finance committee, and other key leaders is important. This task requires that the shared ministry director and team members first have a good grasp of the concept they are advocating. Therefore, the group then needs to spend a significant amount of time learning about shared ministry and immersing itself in resources such as books, videos, websites, denominational efforts, and workshops. (See "Suggested Resources.") The team should also thoroughly investigate other churches with experience in shared ministry.

Once the director and team feel confident that they have a solid understanding of shared ministry, a helpful next step is to put together a rationale outlining what problems shared ministry will solve and how the system will benefit the parish. In gaining support for something new, it is important to explain why the change is needed. What problems does the change address? Why is change necessary and desirable? Because any change is difficult for people to make, the team needs to make a case for why the change is needed in the first place.

This rationale may have been partially created at an earlier stage to justify creating a staff position, in which case the team can use it to create a vision that describes a congregation in which such problems do not exist, in which the shared ministry system is in full flower. A vision describes how the congregation will look after building a shared ministry system.

Some shared ministry committees jump-start their work by hiring an outside consultant knowledgeable in this area, and it is often helpful at this point to invite the consultant to present a workshop to key leaders in the congregation. Early in the planning process, the shared ministry committee and staff person may be only beginning to learn about the system themselves, so often an outside expert will add credibility to the process as well as bring experience and knowledge valuable to the entire community.

The Importance of Using New Language

Another recurring theme in the responses to the informal survey I mentioned at the beginning of the chapter has to do with the need to choose fresh, consistent language for the new vision. Regularly talking about "shared ministry," for example, accomplishes two things. First, the term puts everyone on notice that something new is happening. Second, it ties together all the ideas surfacing because of the unfolding system, thus building a general understanding of the concept in the congregation. When people hear the words *shared ministry*, they will have at least a preliminary idea of what that is about and what some of the system's features might be. The team might also talk about "ministers" instead of "volunteers"; refer to "XYZ Ministry" rather than merely naming the particular work group under discussion (such as the "garden group") or using the term "volunteer team"; and use the phrase "discovering and sharing ones gifts in ministry" instead of "volunteering."

Some who responded to my questions expressed the awareness that early in their development of the shared ministry system they should have made a connection between words traditionally used in the congregation to describe the role of members and the language of shared ministry. For example, congregations frequently use words such as *discipleship* or *stewardship*. Both terms are completely compatible with shared ministry language, but comparing and contrasting these words with the new language is important.

For example, shared ministry builds a system that enables more people to become effective and engaged *disciples*. We become disciples when we follow the teachings and model given to us by Christ. Shared ministry makes it possible for us to live out that discipleship through our participation in the work and mission of the congregation. Similarly, shared ministry is a key component of good stewardship in a congregation. Congregations are called to be stewards of human resources—those gifts of skill, interest, experience, and passion placed in each individual by God. Churches express that stewardship by the way they welcome each individual's contributions to ministry, by the way they help people minister effectively, and by the appreciation they show members. Care for human resources is a necessary and integral part of a stewardship view of church life. No matter what "church speak" is used in your congregation, it will be well worth your while to show how shared ministry works in tandem with the language and concepts already in use.

If this step is neglected, a time will come when a new program or the latest terminology will supplant shared ministry resources and initiatives, under the mistaken notion that shared ministry is an older "program" whose course has run. A well-established shared ministry culture can support new methods of doing strategic planning or assist with a theme of evangelization. It can undergird new educational programs or a congregation-wide emphasis on a particular social justice issue such as homelessness. With its database kept current it can provide important data for doing surveys or for reaching particular segments of the faith community. I would be hard pressed to think of any respected new terminology or program to come along that could not be supported by the concepts and system of shared ministry. The beauty of shared ministry is that it does not have to compete with existing or new programs in a church. It provides the substructure that makes it possible for these programs or ministries to flourish. Shared ministry is not the latest "program" to come along. Rather, it is a system that enables all programs, present and future, to succeed.

Ongoing Tasks for the Shared Ministry Team

The work of the shared ministry team does not cease when the tasks mentioned above are completed. The team will need to assume many ongoing responsibilities to foster continued growth. Aspects of the system will gradually be built, and these will need support, promotion, and explanation, particularly regarding their connection to the system.

Over time the team or committee will undertake many of the following:

1. Casting the vision, educating the parish at large on the big picture of shared ministry. Changing a culture is an ongoing process. You never really complete it, and because congregations are fluid, with people moving in and out, they will always need to renew and recast the vision for those not previously exposed to it.

2. Acting as advisors to and supporters of the director of shared ministry regarding recruitment, matching, and training processes for volunteer ministers. Tasks will multiply for the director of shared ministry as he or she builds the components. Assistance with maintaining existing components and constantly refining them will be one of the team's duties. The team can be invaluable, for example, in updating recruitment and invitation booklets, handling procedures on a recruitment weekend, providing suggestions for a gifts inventory tool, and presenting segments of trainings in specific ministries. Maintenance of existing shared ministry components can be of tremendous help to a director who is trying to concentrate on a new facet of the system.

3. Playing a key role in creating a computer database or another information tracking system; that is, keeping track of people, their gifts, passions, interests, past and present participation in ministry, and so forth. Besides doing the actual data input, committee members can evaluate the effectiveness of the database itself and suggest changes to how data is compiled.

4. Assisting with incorporating new members into the life and community of the church. This might involve periodically organizing and presenting a registration and information event, hosting a welcoming event, providing practical assistance with organizing new members into interest groups, or making

sure they are contacted about ministries they have expressed an interest in.

5. Encouraging retention of current members—caring for them, valuing them, supporting them, and giving them permission to change, grow, try new challenges, and take sabbaticals from current ministry responsibilities. Retention is often related to how well individuals are treated during the course of their ministry involvement. Shared ministry team members can promote respectful and honest recruitment methods, helpful orientation and training, and ways for helping people assess their gifts and match them to ministry opportunities. The team can foster a climate in which congregation members are given permission to say no to a request for help without being made to feel guilty. They can encourage all volunteer ministers to periodically evaluate their own ministry work and how it relates to their spirituality and growth.

6. Engaging in communication efforts, such as acting as liaison to other core groups, ministries, and committees to find out what they are about, what challenges they are facing, and how shared ministry can help.

7. Recognizing the efforts of all the ministries in the church, advocating personalized and individualized appreciation to individuals as well as a community celebration of ministry. The team can offer suggestions for how individualized appreciation could be shown. It could also create an annual congregation appreciation and celebration event.

8. Fostering leadership development through organizing ongoing formation, large group learning experiences, and planning for leadership succession, among other things.

The preparation I have been discussing will take some time to put into place. The unique situation in each congregation will influence whether it will be better first to recruit a director or to invite members into a new shared ministry committee. Individuals' familiarity with basic volunteer management processes will vary, as will their past experiences with ministry in a particular faith community. My suggestions for the ongoing tasks of the shared ministry committee are intended only as a guide. In larger congregations many of these tasks will need to be handed on to new subcommittees, with the committee providing support.

In creating or changing a system, success will depend on how well you prepare the groundwork. Inviting individuals to make up a team and finding a director are two important first steps. Hand in hand with these go forming the team, creating a mission for the team, and casting a vision for the congregation. All this will take some time, but building a committed and knowledgeable group of people who will shepherd the development of a truly life-changing experience for the faith community is invaluable.

CHAPTER 5

Taking the First Steps

O nce the shared ministry team is recruited and a leader selected, the next step is to start the planning process by investigating current volunteer ministry practices. Your initial goal
is to understand what elements of a shared ministry system each
ministry group is already doing well and where the gaps are. As
with discovering what groups of various kinds exist within the
congregation, this investigation will yield surprises. You will find
some ministries have already developed several of the elements of
shared ministry. You will want to capitalize on these examples of
good volunteer management to encourage other ministries that
have few or none of them in place. Leaders and members of ministries who have some elements in place are likely to become supporters for the process generally.

Congregation leaders often suggest doing a parish-wide survey to determine which ministries have various components of an
effective volunteer ministry system in place and where components are missing. At this point, however, I advise shared ministry
teams to survey only staff, board members, ministry leaders, and
ministry members. There are several reasons for keeping the survey narrow. When a congregation member who is not involved in
volunteer ministry is asked to complete a detailed survey evaluating how well the faith community conforms to best practices
for volunteer ministry, the most usual response is "I don't know."
Only members who are active participants in the congregation's
ministry will be able to respond to statements such as "We are
inclusive and have many different ministry opportunities that

appeal to a wide range of ages, interests, gifts, and time availabilities" or "We have an effective system for tracking which volunteers are serving in which ministries." Faced with a preponderance of "I don't know" responses, shared ministry leaders find it difficult to come to any helpful conclusions about the various components, other than the fact that most congregation members are unaware of whether they are in place. Remember, this research is being conducted when the team is just beginning its work and the general membership has received little education about what is happening, the components of an effective volunteer management system, and the goals. A majority of parishioners will need significant education about what an effective volunteer management system looks like before it is appropriate to seek their feedback on these matters. Given the time and resources needed to create, orchestrate, and evaluate a congregation-wide survey, results peppered with "I don't know" answers are likely to be frustrating to everyone.

A survey of this kind also has the potential to generate negativity, because it will probably highlight many elements that are missing from the existing system. Members who are not involved in ministry may conclude that there are big problems with the entire system. For these people, focusing exclusively on the things that are missing or not going well jams a bothersome large stick in the wheel of the cart, which then has to be pulled out before the cart can move on. In my experience, when creating a culture shift in a population, the more positive you can keep the communication and processes, the better.

Further, a parish-wide survey may set expectations for substantial change to occur in an unrealistic time frame. When people don't see the hoped-for change happening quickly, dissatisfaction builds and credibility lessens. Later on in the building process, a congregation-wide survey will be more helpful in guiding planning about how to introduce the new paradigm of shared ministry to the members of the congregation who are not themselves involved in ministries. This is an important step, but one better put into the plan at a later stage.

The team places emphasis on leaders first because they will be the ones bringing shared ministry practices and understanding to the people and volunteer ministries they work with. Staff members will have had experience working with volunteer ministers in their own ministry areas and will probably have a good grasp of congregation-wide systems already in place. They are likely to understand the questions and have thoughts about the answers. Board members, for their part, will have knowledge of the congregation's major volunteer management components such as whether there is a database that tracks ministry participation or an annual event to celebrate the gifts and participation of all volunteer ministers. Ministry members can also give their unique perspective on their experiences, sharing gifts of time and interest within various ministries.

How to Develop a Survey

Developing a survey requires some time to study the elements of a shared ministry system and devise statements with language the respondents will understand. You will have to make decisions about the identifying information you want to collect about each respondent, the format of the questions, and the method for collecting and tabulating the information. It is usually counterproductive to ask respondents to identify themselves by name. Some ministry members may wish to remain anonymous, because they are afraid their answers may displease the leader or staff member. A more important piece of information is the ministry role of the respondent. You need to be able to distinguish which completed surveys have been filled out by staff members, board members, ministry leaders, and members of the ministries. A second important piece of information to have is which ministry or ministry area the respondent is referencing. Begin your survey with a section like the following:

Please indicate what your role is in our congregation's volunteer ministry.

___ I am a member of _____ ministry.

___ I am a staff member for the ministry area of _____.

___ I am responding about ministry in general.

Creating the survey offers an excellent opportunity for the shared ministry team to research important elements of a volunteer management system. Publications from nonprofit organizations on building volunteer management systems can be helpful because there are strong parallels between these systems and shared ministry systems. Books referenced in the "Suggested Resources" section can provide helpful information as well. If other congregations in your area seem to have a good reputation for working with their volunteer ministers, you may find it helpful to interview the leaders and examine any materials they have developed. Area volunteer resource centers or associations of professional directors of volunteers, faith-based or otherwise, are other sources of helpful information.[1] These groups may have developed surveys you can draw on. Having the director of shared ministry or a member of the team join such an association can provide educational and networking opportunities for all the shared ministry leaders.

Designing a survey can offer an opportunity for a congregation member who has experience in this to assist the team. This participation, in turn, brings one more person into contact with the shared ministry concept. It is always a good idea to ask for feedback from several staff members and ministry leaders on the content of a potential survey tool prior to rolling it out. They may identify confusing or poorly worded questions not always apparent to those designing the form. Another way to conduct a survey is to use a Web survey tool such as SurveyMonkey®.

To give you a clearer picture of what a set of questions might look like, figure 5.1 is an example of survey questions relating to the shared ministry component of risk management. It is important to design questions for each component of a shared ministry system—gifts discovery, planning, recruitment, supervision, and so forth. See Jean Trumbauer's *Sharing the Ministry,* listed in "Suggested Resources," for an excellent example of a survey.

1 = We don't do this at all.
5 = We do this very well.
? = I don't know anything about this.

A. We have a written policy approved by our   NA ? 1 2 3 4 5
congregational board regarding the protection
of children and vulnerable adults.
B. We have procedures in place for screening   NA ? 1 2 3 4 5
volunteer ministers who work with people in
high-risk ministries, including reviewing applications,
interviewing, doing background checks, checking
references, and providing training, as applicable.
C. We have procedures in place for how volunteer   NA ? 1 2 3 4 5
ministers work in high-risk ministry areas such
as nursery, faith formation of children and teens,
summer camp programs, and small group meetings
in homes.
D. We have position descriptions for all volunteer   NA ? 1 2 3 4 5
ministers who work in high-risk ministries, and
they are explained to the volunteers.
E. All volunteer ministers who work in high-risk   NA ? 1 2 3 4 5
ministries are supervised by a reliable staff
person or lay leader.
F. We have a system for keeping track of screening   NA ? 1 2 3 4 5
results, supervision processes, and records of
service for all volunteer ministers who work
in high-risk ministries.

Figure 5.1. Example of a Set of Risk Management Questions from a Shared
Ministry Practices Survey

Other Data-Gathering Methods

Besides surveying staff and ministry participants, the director of shared ministry and the shared ministry committee can also interview staff and ministry leaders about their practices. The more thorough and consistent interviewers are (I recommend working from a prepared set of questions), the easier it will be to evaluate the results.

While the main goal is to get an overall picture of how well ministry leaders have put elements of the shared ministry system into place, a secondary goal may be to explore specific details of the individual ministries. This ministry-specific information can be brought back to the shared ministry staff person so that individualized assistance can be provided for these ministry leaders and situations. Individualized help is a watchword in a shared ministry culture. It pays to take advantage of any circumstances that will aid the director or committee in doing this kind of consulting.

The director and committee might also hold focus groups with leaders or with volunteer ministers. Other data to be collected, if possible, includes the total number of parishioners currently involved in all ministries as well as numbers for each individual ministry. If the congregation does not have a central database with this information, gather the information by sending an electronic request to each ministry leader to share the number of people belonging to that ministry. The numbers will have to be compiled by hand. Interviewers can ask if the leaders have noticed any upward or downward trends in those numbers in the past several years.

Analysis of the Research

The purpose of this analysis is to gather information about the existing system so that you can develop a strategy for growing shared ministry and establishing the culture in your congregation.

You can't plan where to go if you don't know where you currently are. An analysis of the survey results can assist the shared ministry team in deciding which components of the shared ministry system need attention first. When examining the data collected, questions to explore are these:

1. Which of the identified components of a shared ministry system already exist, and how well are they functioning?
2. Are there differences in how shared ministers are recruited, appreciated, trained, and so forth, depending on which ministry area or team they serve? If so, what are the differences?
3. Which system components are, in general, poorly carried out?
4. Which system components are entirely missing?
5. From the perspective of the individual ministry member, what has the person's experience serving in a specific ministry been like?
6. What problems do ministry leaders identify with regard to volunteer ministry experience in each area of service?

A simultaneous analysis of survey results from the leaders and the ministry members will indicate where discrepancies may exist between the volunteer minister's actual experiences and what the leader of a particular ministry reports. The results of this comparison can further shape the plans and set priorities for the shared ministry team and director. For example, if the staff member for a particular ministry evaluates the training component as very good and the ministry members rate it as low, then a comprehensive evaluation of member training may be needed. A task group from the ministry, which includes the staff member, can complete the evaluation. Or if ministry members express difficulty connecting their ministry participation to a sense of God's presence in their lives and the staff member believes this connection is strong, then there is a disconnect between what the staff person perceives and what the ministry member actually experiences. The shared ministry director can review the results of the survey with the staff person and suggest ways to handle the disconnect. The review may lead the staff member and ministry members to reexamine and restructure how this component is dealt with, so that volunteer ministers will be better prepared, supported, and more effective in their work.

One goal of this information-gathering phase is to discover not only the actual level of development of volunteer ministry practices but also whether ministry leaders consider the various components of a shared ministry system in their work or even know about them. If so, what is their assessment of the effectiveness with which these are carried out in ministries? From leaders' answers, it is possible to infer the level of sophistication they have about working with volunteer ministries. Do they already have many shared ministry components built into their groups? For example, do they have position descriptions for each ministry? Are screening processes in place for volunteers who work with children's ministries? Are training sessions offered to new members of the ministry? If so, then the team will not need to spend a great amount of time familiarizing the leaders with the basic principles. On the other hand, if the answers to the survey questions indicate a majority of leaders are unfamiliar with best practices in working with volunteers, the team and director of shared ministry will have to start with some intensive education to bring people up to speed. In addition, if the same system component seems to be missing or presenting challenges in many ministries, shared ministry leaders might decide to make that specific component a high priority.

Trends in the number of participants in a congregation's ministries can also be revealing. Declining numbers in a particular ministry can indicate volunteer management issues. The ministry may need to be restructured to meet changing needs in the congregation. If many ministries have declining numbers, that information will suggest a broader strategy. If a specific ministry is seeing a significant increase in volunteer ministers, the shared ministry director and team can look at what the ministry is doing right and use this as a model for other ministries.

As well as providing you with valuable information for planning, surveying and interviewing leaders and staff offer a number of side benefits. In the course of answering the questions, people are learning what the key points of shared ministry are. They are being exposed to new language and to a picture of a comprehensive system for encouraging participation in the church's ministries. You are setting expectations for developing the system as well. All these benefits will assist you in growing this new culture.

Creating a Plan

Based on the results of the study, the shared ministry director and committee create an initial one- or two-year plan. Include big picture goals in the plan as well as small steps needed to accomplish those goals. As with any well-thought-out plan, include action steps with time lines, who is responsible for working on the step, and checkpoints along the way. Figure 5.2 on page 62 shows an example of a partial plan.

In my experience, most congregations appropriately decide to tackle recruitment first. Generally a lack of volunteers is a key complaint that leads a faith community to look for help with shared ministry. From a strategic standpoint, if the church leaders as a whole express strong concern about the few people participating in ministry, or if burnout is prevalent among ministry volunteers, then addressing this felt need will generate lots of payoffs to the culture-building effort. Congregation members will view the shared ministry committee and director as being responsive to the needs of the congregation. (See chapter 6 for a comprehensive discussion of recruitment.)

Goal for Year 1: To create a shared ministry database for
tracking each member's participation in ministry.

Objective 1:
Determine what fields need to be included in the database.

Action Step 1: Recruit a small team to investigate samples of ministry
participation databases from other congregations of a similar size.
Responsible parties: Shared Ministry Team members Sue Smith and
John Doe
Completion date: February 15

Action Step 2: Obtain sample databases from software companies.
Responsible parties: Members of the investigative team (to be filled in
after they are recruited)
Completion date: April 1

Action Step 3: Analyze sample databases and compile
recommendations for what to include in our shared ministry
database.
Responsible parties: Members of the investigative team
Completion date: June 1

Objective 2:
Design the database.

Action Step 1: Recruit a qualified database programmer, from within
the congregation if possible.
Responsible parties: Members of a subcommittee of the Shared
Ministry Team
Completion date: May 1

Figure 5.2. Example of Partial Shared Ministry Plan

Occasionally a congregation will decide to focus first on an appreciation event for all its current volunteer ministers or a general celebration of all the ministry work of the faith community. Tying this event to an appropriate liturgical season, sermon series, or worship experience draws a connection for church members between the theological beliefs of the community and the role of shared ministry in living out those beliefs. This type of event can be used to publicize the new shared ministry initiative and the shared ministry leadership team sponsoring it. It can become the kickoff to the entire first year of building shared ministry. (See chapter 7 for a more in-depth discussion of appreciation and celebration.)

Each congregation is a unique entity. Many other areas could be selected to work on first. But recruitment and an appreciation event are the most frequently chosen. As you will see in the chapters that follow, many other components of shared ministry will be brought into play when doing comprehensive planning for recruitment or ministry appreciation. Whatever the shared ministry team selects as its first focus, the emphasis should (1) be significant enough to be noticed by the congregation, (2) address a felt need of the congregational leadership, and (3) be achievable in some measureable way. With these three criteria in place, you stand a good chance of being successful in this all-important first initiative for shared ministry. Success at the beginning will bring big rewards later by building the credibility of the shared ministry staff person and the team. It will generate goodwill and encourage participation in the next stages of the process. The next two chapters go into detail about the recruitment and appreciation elements as options for initial focus.

CHAPTER 6

Doing a Churchwide
Recruitment Drive

I magine you are relatively new to a faith community. One
weekend the congregation holds a recruitment event to get
more members involved in the ministries of that church. You
are pretty new to the area. You joined this congregation, hoping
that membership would give you an opportunity to get to know
some people in the community. You have been attending services
fairly regularly and have heard bits and pieces from time to time
about some of the groups involved in the church. But you really
have only a fuzzy, incomplete picture of what goes on in this faith
community.

Or imagine that although you have been a member of this
congregation for quite a while, you just haven't gotten around to
joining any ministry yet. Now something seems to be nudging you
to move out of your safety zone and give volunteering a try. Gathering up your courage, you look over the ministry opportunity
sheet put in your pew and gamely check off a couple of ministries
that look interesting.

The recruitment forms are collected at the end of the service,
and you go home to wait for a call. And you wait. And you wait.
And you wait. Several weeks go by, then a month, then several
months. At a certain point, unless you are extremely patient, you
write off the exercise as just another reason you haven't gotten involved in anything at the parish in the first place.

If you were really excited to get involved, you feel let down. Apparently this church has no need of additional helpers, despite the plea from the pulpit that the pastor so eloquently made. You guess that this congregation really isn't interested in adding anyone new to its committees and teams. Or you wonder, was the reason you weren't contacted something about you personally? Do people not like you? Do they think you don't have much to offer them in the way of gifts and talents? Is it because of your skin color, your educational level, or your economic status? Maybe you don't know the right people, are not part of the "in" crowd. Such feelings of rejection, alienation, anger, and hurt engendered by this failure to connect after a recruitment campaign can simmer for many years and create cynicism and disengagement, the opposite of what the congregation intended by offering the event.

Preparing for Recruitment

Creating some sort of sign-up form and a process for distributing it is not enough. What is also needed is a system for capturing the information coming in and following up on it. Many congregations say their biggest challenge is that not enough people are involved in their ministries. Yet a common mistake churches make when conducting a recruitment drive is that they try to put it on before they have sufficiently prepared. You can do more harm than good if you attempt to do a full congregation recruitment and don't have procedures in place to follow up with people who express a desire to join a ministry.

In planning a recruitment event, a church generally needs to spend the better part of a year preparing. This sounds like a long time, but my experience has shown that if the congregation is starting to build a shared ministry system from ground zero, it will take that long to do all the foundational work to ensure a successful recruitment.

Designing and carrying out an effective recruitment effort depends on a solid partnership between two types of people: big-picture thinkers, who maintain a clear sense of the goal and offer their support and encouragement, and detail-oriented people, who will work out the required organizational processes. Both groups must grasp the scope and magnitude of the work required to complete this planning and design. If they collaborate, they can accomplish this challenging and rewarding task.

The following tasks need to be accomplished as preparation for conducting an effective recruitment effort:

1. Compile a list of all groups in your church.
2. Determine which groups exist primarily to serve others and which are more focused on fellowship, education, or support services.
3. Gather existing position descriptions for current ministries, and edit them according to an agreed-upon format.
4. Design a process for creating position descriptions for all those ministries that don't currently have one.
5. Design a recruitment event, and set a target date.
6. Create a ministry recruitment form or catalog that contains information on each ministry, and make a sign-up sheet. Plan a distribution process.
7. Evaluate tracking tools available through your congregation's membership management software as well as other available software.
8. Select and prepare the chosen software to receive the data to be collected.
9. Design a follow-up process to ensure people who fill out a sign-up form and turn it in will be contacted about their interest.
10. Brief all congregation leaders, paid and volunteer, regarding the recruitment process and expectations for their participation.
11. Publicize the recruitment event.
12. Recruit and train data-entry volunteers.

STEP 1: COMPILE A LIST OF ALL CHURCH GROUPS

The director of shared ministry, the shared ministry team, or a combination of the two can work together on compiling a list of all groups in the church. Groups might be referred to as teams, committees, ministries, task forces, classes, care teams, small groups, clubs, support groups, and small Christian communities. An established congregation will have many groups that perform a variety of functions. Typically, some groups focus on service to individual members or to the congregation as a whole. Examples are religious education teachers and assistants, building cleaners, gardeners, ushers, and choirs. Other groups provide social opportunities for specific segments of the church population or for people with particular interests. Baseball teams, scout groups, seniors' book clubs, and new parents' night-out groups are examples of these. Still others support people experiencing grief, divorce, chronic illnesses, or addictions. Most congregations are amazed by the number and variety of groups that are part of the congregation. They are also surprised to discover groups that few people, including staff members and pastors, realize even exist!

Because your goal is to change the culture of the faith community, it is important to learn who will be affected by the changes most directly. Questions planners need to ask are these:

- What groups do we have in this church?
- What is each group's function?
- How many people belong to each group?
- Who is the leader or contact person for the group?

STEP 2: IDENTIFY EACH GROUP'S PRIMARY FOCUS

A common question in congregations that are developing a shared ministry system is, what is ministry? Consequently, an important part of creating a shared ministry culture is educating the entire membership about what *ministry* means. An important step is to clarify which groups in the congregation fit under that term's umbrella and which focus primarily on support, study, or fellowship.

In a shared ministry culture, *ministry* is generally understood as congregation-sponsored service, whether to members of the congregation or to people outside the faith community. Teaching religious education classes, assisting with worship, singing in the choir, visiting sick and shut-in members, collecting food for the food shelf, and the like are ways of serving within the congregation. Similarly, working with a group representing your congregation on a Habitat for Humanity house and acting as a congregation representative on a community-based committee addressing race discrimination are examples of ministries outside the walls of the congregation. By the term *outside the walls*, I am referring to ministry that serves people who are not members of the congregation. Generally, congregations have a combination of groups, some of which minister to members and others that serve out in the community.

Some groups are not ministries per se. For example, the monthly bridge group and the men's annual fishing trip group would generally be classified as social groups. Their focus is on fellowship opportunities. While an individual may benefit greatly from participation in such a group—and that is a good thing—the group itself is not intended to be a *ministry*. On the other hand, the purpose of a ministry might be to offer fellowship opportunities for people with a particular need; for example, to offer a social outlet for developmentally challenged young adults. In this case, those who facilitate the events would be considered ministers, and their positions would be classified as a ministry. Developmentally challenged young adults who wish to participate in the social activities are not the ministers; rather, they are the receivers of the ministry efforts.

What about groups that fall into gray areas? A lot of fellowship groups would be in this category. Fellowship and community-building groups are important to the life of the faith community, no question. The heart of the matter, however, is whether the fellowship group focuses most of its effort on social opportunities or is mainly focused on serving the community. If the latter, it is a ministry.

Just as some groups are ministries and others are not, within a group are many roles, meaning some participants are ministers and some are not. The organizers and facilitators of support groups would qualify as ministers, while the people who join a group because they are looking for help in a difficult situation are members of the support group itself. Leaders and facilitators of a young parents' education and fellowship group can be considered ministers because they are organizing, leading, and assisting with educational opportunities. The young couples who want to become part of the fellowship small group but take no part in organization, leadership, or arranging for educational experiences are not actually serving; rather, they are the ones being served by those leaders and organizers.

The men's Saturday morning donuts-and-coffee fellowship gathering that holds several fundraisers during the year to assist with the congregation's needs is both fellowship and ministry based. It would seem logical to include them in a ministry listing because of their fund-raising efforts. Meals-on-wheels drivers are a ministry group. They deliver the meals and are thus providing a service to the community, but the people who receive the meals are being served by the ministry and are not part of the ministry group. An adult faith formation series will involve people who facilitate discussion groups, handle hospitality, and present information—all volunteer ministers. People who attend the series to learn but do not assist with the process are not considered volunteer ministers. Similarly people attending the annual parish picnic are not performing a ministry. All the various teams working at the event—overseeing setup, food stands, games, cakewalk, and the like—are performing a ministry for the faith community.

The distinction between ministry groups and other types of groups will be important when you design your recruitment form. There are two reasons for being consistent about the difference, one practical and one strategic. First, you want to ensure people understand whether they would be joining a group as a receiver of service or as a member of the ministry that provides the service. Those wanting to join a support group to obtain help, for example, would not sign up to be a member of that ministry. Opportunities to *organize and facilitate* a support, study, or fellowship group would be listed as openings for *ministry*.

Ideally, the term *recruitment* is not used for the process of gathering names of individuals who wish to participate in a group. The term is appropriate for gathering names of people who would like to volunteer to lead the group in some way. Some congregations create a separate form people use to indicate interest in joining a support, study, or fellowship group as a participant. Others simply list various types of opportunities on a single form. If you choose to include everything in one booklet or form, be sure to distinguish clearly between *ministry* opportunities and other sections that list support services available from the congregation, such as 12-step groups, a food shelf, spiritual counseling, and the like; educational opportunities, such as classes for children or special speakers for adults; and fellowship opportunities.

There is also a strategic reason for not mixing all types of groups in a single booklet or form. Remember that this whole process of recruiting people into ministry in an organized way may be unfamiliar to the congregation. Some staff or lay members may have fears that the shared ministry committee is trying to take over their ministry or group, particularly when the shared ministry committee collects names of people needing support or wishing to attend a study class. Leaders of a particular ministry may feel this is part of their responsibility and wish to deal directly with the people to be served. The very fact that the shared ministry committee is collecting this information can be threatening to the group's leaders. Fears will ease when the committee is able to provide names of new ministry members for the leaders of a ministry group. But keeping track of other kinds of information specific to the ministry, such as lists of people being served, deflects the shared ministry committee from its purpose, which is growing the ministry of the congregation.

STEP 3: GATHER POSITION DESCRIPTIONS

The next step is to gather existing position descriptions for current ministries and edit them according to an agreed-upon format. It often takes some detective work to locate existing position descriptions, but when you do find them, it is best to edit them in partnership with members of the given ministry, even if they have never seen the job descriptions before. They are the ones who know the ministry most intimately and can tell you how closely the existing description corresponds to the actual work being done. They also are in a good position to tell you what gifts, responsibilities, and time commitments are important.

These questions will guide your investigation:

- Which ministry groups have written position descriptions for their work?
- How specific, accurate, and comprehensive are they?
- Where are they located? Is the ministry's position description written down and kept in a file somewhere? Is it on a staff member or lay leader's computer?
- Does the church have any history of documenting position descriptions for all its various ministries in some central place? Where are these located? Compiled in a notebook, in a computer file?
- Does the ministry operate from an unwritten or assumed position description? If so, what do the leaders identify as key elements of this unwritten position description?
- Do the lay ministers ever see these descriptions? Are the descriptions regularly used in recruitment and supervision?

It takes time and lots of patience to search out the answers to all these questions. Depending on the size of the congregation, many shared ministry committees and directors of shared ministry can spend months visiting with every group in their church, gathering copies of existing position descriptions, and reviewing them for their completeness, accuracy, and uniformity. Combining this search with the introductory visit to become acquainted with the ministries saves you valuable time and effort.

The magnitude of the job is one reason it often takes almost a year to prepare for an effective recruitment drive. A good many churches will not have any written position descriptions for their ministries. Some may have rudimentary descriptions for ministries related to worship, sacramental, or board positions. You may find that long ago, someone did compile or write descriptions for a number of ministries. However, upon closer examination, you might find that some of these ministries no longer exist or have changed dramatically, so the descriptions are no longer accurate. A few ministries might have done a good job creating position descriptions that only need a little tweaking to conform to a new format.

The shared ministry team and director need to design a standard format that can be used for all position descriptions. Below is a list of possible components of a position description.[1]

Position title
Purpose of position and connection to mission of the
    congregation
Responsibilities
Gifts and qualifications
Amount of time required
When ministry is performed
Length of commitment
Screening requirements
Training and support provided
Responsible to
Date last reviewed

STEP 4: DESIGN A PROCESS FOR CREATING NEW POSITION
DESCRIPTIONS

Some current ministries will not have position descriptions, so
the next step is to design a process for creating new position descriptions for all those ministries. Especially if your congregation
is a large one, you can use current position descriptions for your
first year's recruitment efforts. That gives you twelve more months
to gather information, create, and edit position descriptions for
all the ministries for the next year's recruitment process. An advantage to this method is that you can more quickly get your recruitment efforts up and running. A disadvantage is that these
descriptions will not be uniformly available, clear, and helpful.
Congregations will generally tolerate this lack of uniformity for
the first year or two. After that, it begins to chip away at the per-
ception that an actual system is being created and instead leaves
the impression that it's a haphazard attempt to do a few things
differently. My advice is to try to get all position descriptions completed before the recruitment event, if at all possible.

Position descriptions are important for many reasons, including the following:[2]

- Position descriptions show respect for volunteers' time.
- Position descriptions ensure volunteers know what is expect-
  ed of them.
- Position descriptions help match gifts and ministries.
- Position descriptions are aids in planning.
- Position descriptions are recruiting tools.
- Position descriptions are evaluation tools.
- Position descriptions are aids in minimizing risk.

Position descriptions show respect for volunteers' time. Time is the
most precious thing people possess these days. It can be worth as
much or more to them than money. Without a position description, responsibilities and expectations can seem overwhelming to

already incredibly busy people. Next to failure to follow up with someone who has offered his or her gifts of time and skill, the second most likely reason for a lack of interest in a ministry is the absence of a good operational position description.

Position descriptions ensure volunteers know what is expected of them. Without concise position descriptions, individuals recruited for a position often do not have a clear understanding of what is actually involved. Later they find out that the job consists of much more than they are prepared to handle. Or an individual may turn down a position because he is afraid it will go on forever or that it will involve him in an increasingly greater number of responsibilities. Sometimes individuals who have not been given a position description are criticized for not carrying out everything in a position, even though no one ever told them exactly what they were expected to do.

Position descriptions help match gifts and ministries. Without accurate position descriptions, volunteers may be woefully mismatched to a ministry, perform poorly, or handle their responsibilities in a dangerous fashion, because they lack an understanding of exactly what the position requires. Position descriptions can help correct all these problems.

Position descriptions are aids in planning. A well-written position description helps to connect the work of the ministry to its own goals and to the mission of the church. A ministry position that is intimately connected to the goals and purposes of the congregation is a valuable unifying tool. It addresses questions such as these:

- What are our ministry goals?
- What tasks must be accomplished to reach those goals?
- How does this position contribute to our ministry goals?

- How does this position contribute to the mission of this church?
- What are the responsibilities of the person who holds this position?
- What gifts will enable a person to succeed in this position?
- What screening requirements, if any, are there?
- What is the time commitment?

Position descriptions are recruiting tools. A position description helps to encourage the right people to offer their gifts. They can compare the position's responsibilities, the gifts helpful for this ministry, and the skills and time required to determine if the needs match what they have to offer. The presence of a position description also builds trust and credibility. It tells the volunteer minister that the work of this ministry has been well thought out. Finally, it affirms the value of both the ministry and the volunteer. In a faith community where position descriptions are the accepted mode of operating, people will make comments such as, "This place is organized," "This must be an important job," "I am important," "I need to take this seriously," "I'm impressed with this church and its ministries."

Position descriptions are evaluation tools. A position description becomes a tool to provide honest, objective feedback to individuals. Volunteer ministers can reflect on their activity in the ministry and see how well they were able to meet the expectations and responsibilities listed in the position description. Leaders and supervisors can use it to discuss problems with behavior or to praise and affirm excellent work in the ministry.

The position description can also become a helpful tool for evaluating a ministry's work. Staff, leaders, and ministry members might ask, Are we addressing the mission effectively? Is our work organized in such a way that people can contribute efficiently and effectively? Are responsibilities and expectations reasonable?

Position descriptions are aids in minimizing risk. By setting bound-aries for the work—what is and what is not included in the job—and listing training and screening requirements, a good position description contributes to the safety of all those involved in giving and receiving ministry.

The existence of a well-written description assures a poten-tial volunteer that the ministry is well organized and that she or he will not be overwhelmed with unexpected responsibilities. It ensures that gifted people will be serving with enthusiasm in the areas of their giftedness and contributing wonderful things to the mission of the church.

Creating the Position Description

It is not the responsibility of the director of shared ministry or the shared ministry team to write all position descriptions. Rather, they promote the writing and provide models and assistance to staff members and ministry groups, who are responsible for writ-ing position descriptions for the ministries they are involved in.

The following steps can assist you in creating position descriptions.

Assist all existing ministries with creating or redoing the cur-rent ministry position descriptions to fit the new uniform format. You might meet with ministry leaders during meetings they have already scheduled. Another method is to call together represen-tatives from all ministries from a given area, such as liturgy and worship or religious education, to work on this task together. In small congregations, a "position description writing night" for all ministries can be called. In all cases, the shared ministry team or staff person can present the new format, the rationale for it, and examples of good position descriptions to use as models. Mem-bers of the shared ministry team can circulate around the room and assist individual ministries with writing good descriptions.

In some instances the shared ministry director or a shared ministry team member may meet one-on-one with a ministry leader to assist him or her in writing the descriptions. E-mail can be used to provide examples of the new format and to submit completed position descriptions to the director of shared ministry.

The shared ministry staff person and team members should create a follow-up process to ensure each ministry has a position description well before the recruitment drive begins. Gather copies of all descriptions in one computer file for ease in reviewing and keeping track of changes. Following up with ministries to make sure they have completed their position descriptions is difficult if there is no centralized place for compiling them. Many congregations also put all their position descriptions on their websites so that members can read them and gain a good understanding of each ministry before choosing ones to participate in.

As you can see, this whole process can take many months to complete, but all the time and effort will be worth it in the end. As you interact with the various staff and ministry leaders, you raise awareness of shared ministry. You also build relationships and trust between you, the shared ministry team, and the rest of the congregation.

I was recently discussing position descriptions at a gathering of directors of volunteers. One of the participants had taken a training course from me several years ago, when she was new to the field. She stated that the one regret she had was that she hadn't followed my recommendation and made sure position descriptions were written for every ministry at the very start. She now realizes how much further she would have come if she had started with this task. A consistent lack of position descriptions throughout the system means that members will encounter varying degrees of helpful information about what their jobs are and what the ministry is all about. A lack of a standard process means that the director will need to address issues of missing or inaccurate position descriptions on a case-by-case basis, convincing each individual ministry leader about the necessity for having them. This can be very time consuming. Each time a volunteer minister has a confusing or difficult time getting involved, there is the potential for a loss of credibility for the shared ministry team and the process itself. Requesting the pastor to provide enthusiastic verbal support for the process communicates to ministry leaders the importance of their participation, including writing position descriptions.

STEP 5: DESIGN THE EVENT AND SET THE DATE

So far we have been examining the groundwork that must be laid prior to the recruitment event itself. Next, we will look at the steps involved in creating the actual event. I have found that developing an annual recruitment event tied to a particular worship weekend is a helpful way to organize and introduce the process. Using weekend worship brings the largest number of people together at one time, thus ensuring you will reach as many members as possible. An annual event helps to build the culture as people experience the cyclical nature of committing or recommitting to participation in ministry. People will begin to get the connection between the term *shared ministry* and one of its important parts— recruitment. Placing the recruitment event within the worship service connects it to the faith and spirituality of the congregation. This kind of service speaks directly to the theology that all Christians are called through baptism to share their gifts with the congregation. Further, a worship service offers a unique opportunity for the congregation to see the importance the pastor places on participation in ministry as a right and responsibility for all believers. Music, homilies, even the decoration of the worship space itself can point to this central theme.

Current ministry members might share their stories with the congregation about the value to them personally of participating in ministry. A personal statement specific to the individual is much more engaging than listing values that are not personally experienced. Some congregations show a video of members engaged in ministry. In some congregations, people fill out recruitment forms at a specific point in the worship service. Ushers can collect them and at an appropriate time bring them forward in baskets as a symbol that members are offering their gifts to God and the community.

The information that follows is based on the premise that the recruitment event will take place at a weekend worship service.

STEP 6: CREATE AND DISTRIBUTE RECRUITMENT RESOURCES

Prior to the event, you will need to create a ministry recruitment form or catalog that contains information on each ministry and a sign-up sheet. Plan a distribution process. This task provides an excellent opportunity to utilize the gifts and talents of a member of the shared ministry committee or another church member. This person should have skill and experience working with desktop publishing software, layout, and design. A few congregations have paid staff that can perform this function as well. However, including a congregation member, or even a committee of members, in the design of the catalog provides an opportunity to help more people understand and get involved in the work of shared ministry. Even if no one on the committee has the needed skills to design it, the shared ministry committee can provide suggestions and general direction for creating a form and give final approval.

Typically the *recruitment form* will categorize all ministry opportunities by group—for example, social justice ministries, music ministries, teen ministries, and so forth. If the church does not have an organizational chart showing ministry areas, leaders need to be encouraged to create such a chart. Preparing for a recruitment weekend provides an excellent opportunity for the leaders to tackle such a task. However, if the recruitment form is logically designed, you do not need to wait for an official organizational chart to be created before moving ahead with designing the form.

Each ministry listed should have a two- to three-sentence description of the main responsibilities of the ministry, for inclusion in the catalog or on the form. People need to have an idea of what the Donut Sunday team does, for example. Make the donuts? Buy the donuts? Set out the donuts? Eat the donuts? Clean up after the event?

The best way to develop these descriptions is to enlist the help of the staff and lay leaders who work with each ministry. Making a personal visit to each group is often the best way to establish a good working relationship. The director of shared ministry or a team member can explain the concept of shared ministry, what some of its components are, and how the groups can benefit by participating in a congregation-wide recruitment event. Providing sample descriptions so that people will understand what you are asking for is helpful. The following are examples:

> *Befriender Ministry*: Through monthly home visits, offer support and friendship to an individual experiencing chronic illness, loss of a loved one, or other life challenge. Schedule is flexible. Background check, training, and monthly peer supervision meetings required.
>
> *Liturgy Commission*: Develop a vision for the focus and themes of seasons of community worship and create long-range plans and policies; encourage full involvement of the community in worship. Six two-hour meetings per year. Knowledge of liturgical practices needed.
>
> *Sunday School Co-Catechist*: Partner with another catechist to gather with five to seven children, ages three to five years, for one hour a week. Classes are held during the Sunday 8:00 a.m. and 10:00 a.m. worship services. Help children learn about and share their faith through lessons, activities, Scripture, and prayer. September through April. Training provided.

As obvious as the ministry tasks seem to you and the ministry team, remember that many church members have no history of volunteer ministry with your parish, and they need to be told explicitly what happens in that ministry.

Keeping in mind that you will want to keep track of each person's recruitment information on a computer, and that you will want to be able to run reports concerning data on specific individuals, ministries, or groups of ministries, you will also need to establish some numbering system for digitally identifying each individual and ministry. Thus every ministry needs to have a unique code. Depending on the type of software you use, this is usually a series of letters and numbers that are linked to the particular ministry. Each ministry has a name as well, but for ease of designing reports and calling up data, a ministry code is very helpful. You will find that ministries can change their names or become inactive and new ones created as the focus and responsibilities change or when a new staff leader is hired. Teen ministry may be called "Youth for Christ" one year, "Small Group Teen Ministry" for the next several years, and "Teens Share Faith" the next year. If you want to do a report showing how many youth participated over seven years in the teen ministry program, it is much easier to use one code number as opposed to having to find or remember and enter three different names for the same ministry. The codes also make for ease and speed of entry into the database.

The *sign-up form* should be simple and easy to understand. Depending on the number of ministries in your church, a sheet of paper, perhaps colored, with the ministries, codes, and descriptions listed on the front and back is fine. Provide a space for the individual's name and contact information and a way for members to indicate the specific ministries they are interested in. They could check boxes, write on lines, or circle the ministry name. See figure 6.1 for an example of a simple recruitment form.[3]

In future years you can tweak the form to include additional information that would be helpful or to reorganize the ministry listings. Watching the evolution of a recruitment tool from a single sheet of paper to a booklet is one of the rewarding parts of working on shared ministry. Each year you have a chance to perfect the tool a bit more.

Some experienced and larger churches print professional-looking booklets, in color and on special paper, with photos of people participating in each ministry and detailed information about screening and other requirements. The descriptions might indicate which ministries are appropriate for teens or families. There may be check boxes to indicate whether the person signing up is new to the ministry or returning. In addition to the ministry

Cliff Lake Congregational Church
5001 Lakeside Drive
Any City, Any State 12345

Shared Ministry
Volunteer Opportunities
Fall 2012

Cliff Lake Congregational Church is more than just Sunday mornings. These volunteer opportunities open up new doors to becoming better acquainted with your church and meeting other church friends.

We invite you to contribute your gifts of time, interest, and skills to any of our ministry areas. The volunteer ministry positions include both one-time commitments as well as longer term opportunities. If you wish to participate, please check one or more areas of interest and return this form as soon as possible to Cliff Lake Church, Attention: Shared Ministry Team

Our promise to you:

1. Your response will be appreciated because you and these activities are important to the life of the church.
2. The Shared Ministry Team will acknowledge your interest by e-mail or letter within two weeks.
3. We will seek a place for all who indicate their willingness to help.

Name _____
Address _____
City/State _____ Zip _____
Email _____ Telephone (home) _____
Telephone (work) _____ Adult ___ Teen ___ Child ___

Please fill out one form per person. Additional copies of this brochure will be available at the 8:30 and 10:30 church services on Sunday, September 10, and also in the church office.

Nursery Helpers: Assist others in caring for children ages five months to five years while parents are at worship or ministry meetings. Includes unstructured play and snack. Requires previous experience with young children and gifts of playfulness and imagination. Flexible scheduling to meet your availability. 2 hours Sunday mornings or weekday evenings. Must have background check.

Church School Music Director: Coordinate music program for church school. Select and teach music to children ages three to eleven. Knowledge of church music, ability to play piano, and skills working with children required. Two-and-one-half hours Sunday mornings 10:30 to 11:45, plus preparation time. September 30 to June 2. Background check and references required.

Donut Sunday Helpers: As part of a team of six, pour coffee, juice and serve donuts after services Sunday morning. Clean fellowship hall afterward. Time commitment forty-five minutes after each service, Sundays throughout the year. Flexible scheduling to meet your availability. Great family ministry opportunity.

Church School Resources Room Helpers: Check attendance at Church School, keep teachers supplied with craft materials, keep resource room orderly, purchase supplies, monitor halls during classes. Organizational skills and interest in children and education important. Two hours weekly on Sunday mornings 10:00 to noon. September 30 to June 2. Flexible schedule. Orientation, support, and supervision provided by Church School Director. Background check required.

Figure 6.1. Sample Recruitment Form

Program Support

___ Monday Night Volunteers: Participate in recreation program for adults with developmental disabilities. Play games, assist with crafts. Patient, friendly personalities needed. Three hours, Monday evening 6:00 to 9:00 pm; help from one to four Monday nights per month. September to June. Program coordinators present to orient and direct activities.

___ Meals on Wheels: Deliver up to six meals to homebound within 20-mile radius of church one Thursday each month, 11:00 to noon. Volunteer with a friend or work alone. Background check required. Must provide your own car.

___ New Member Orientation and Registration Team: Present a 20 minute welcome and overview of Cliff Lake Church and its programs to new members. Assist with registration paperwork. Provide hospitality and refreshments for 4 to 6 people. Alternate months starting with January. Outlines and scripts are provided. Public speaking ease and familiarity with Cliff Lake programs necessary. Training provided.

___ Greeters for Sunday Service: Graciously greet people as they enter the church for 10:30 service. Give directions and answer questions, 10:00 to 10:30 am, one or more Sundays September through June.

___ Cliff Lake Teen Fellowship Team: Work with director of teen programs to plan and attend four fellowship events yearly. Comfortable around and interested in high-school-aged young people. Must attend orientation and have background check completed.

Office Support

___ Office Receptionist: Assist office staff by greeting people who come to the office, answering telephones, and taking messages. Three hour block of time between 8:30 and 4:45 Monday – Friday, one or more times per month. Three to six month commitment.

___ Education Materials Prep Helpers: Copy, collate, and assemble packets of educational materials for religious education teachers. Two hours weekly on either Monday afternoon or Tuesday evening.

Church Environment

___ Maintenance Team: Work with others to do simple repair projects, paint, mow lawns, shovel snow, rake leaves, deep clean carpets. Saturdays from 9 to 12 noon. Flexible scheduling.

___ Worship Space Decorators: work with staff to prepare worship space for special holidays, and seasons. Quarterly planning meetings and four to six Saturdays prior to the holiday or start of a new season. Material will be purchased by Cliff Lake. All visual artistic gifts and experience welcome.

___ Flower Committee: Work in pairs to create individual arrangements from sanctuary flowers for homebound members following Sunday services. Approximate time required — 30 minutes, six to eight times a year on rotating schedule. Additional time requested during Advent and Easter.

Figure 6.1. Sample Recruitment Form (continued)

information, many include a tear-off sign-up sheet or two attached in the booklet. Members signing up can explore all the ministries of interest to them, pull out the sign-up sheet, fill it in, and return it to the congregation. Some congregations list the staff liaison for each ministry and how to contact the person. Congregations are now starting to put their forms online so that they are accessible via the church website. (For an excellent example of a comprehensive sophisticated recruitment catalog, go to the website www.sjn. org.) Figure 6.2 and figure 6.3 can be found on the Alban website at www.alban.org/sharedministry/.[4] There you will find an example of a ministry sign up form from a large congregation (figure 6.2) and a page of minsitry descriptions from a recruitment booklet (figure 6.3).

As with the recruitment form, you will be able to create a more sophisticated brochure over time as you identify what information is most valuable both for you and for members of the congregation.

Printing and Distributing the Recruitment Form Affordably

The most obvious way to fund the recruitment forms is to build the expense into the annual shared ministry budget. This option speaks volumes about the commitment of the church to the value of the shared ministry system. Congregations that include advertising in their bulletin or worship folder may find that for any project the congregation chooses, some bulletin publishing companies will print a certain number of pages for free, based on the number of advertisers. Or a member or small group of shared ministry enthusiasts could be asked to cover the printing and mailing costs. A printer who is a member of the parish may be willing to print the forms at little or no cost. All these options need to be explored and decisions made as part of the initial planning process. The shared ministry team can assist with this work in partnership with the staff, liturgy planners, ministry leaders, and shared ministry staff person.

The question of how to distribute the recruitment form and do it affordably is important to figure out. There are many options. One way is to include it in the regularly distributed church newsletter or weekly worship bulletin. This saves you the cost of postage for an additional mailing. However, larger booklets will need to be mailed separately. Putting the ministry information and sign-up form on the congregation's website is a way to get the attention of your technically savvy members and costs nothing.

Having recruitment forms permanently available in the congregation's gathering spaces is important in order to reach people who are new or who were absent on the weekend the forms were handed out. Ahead of the annual recruitment event, providing all ministry leaders with a number of recruitment forms to pass out to their ministry members at their next gathering can also be helpful. Sometimes longstanding members of a ministry may be the most difficult to persuade to fill out a ministry form. They point to the fact that they have been members of the ministry for many years and everyone knows they are involved already. Distributing forms to these longstanding ministry members, as well as all members of established ministries, well ahead of the recruitment event provides you with an opportunity to talk with them about shared ministry as a culture change. You can explain that processes for becoming involved in ministry are standardized and commitment to a ministry is made on a yearly basis. Current ministry members can be an example, encouraging others to participate in the new process by filling out a sign-up form. This method of distribution can lead to a much better response from some of the most dedicated ministers.

Some larger parishes mail their annual recruitment booklets and ask members to look them over several weeks ahead of the recruitment event. Members have the option of returning the recruitment sign-up form prior to the weekend event or on that weekend when they attend services. Obviously, you will accept any recruitment forms turned in at any time. But it is much simpler and easier for ministries to plan if they have a majority of their members on board at the beginning of the fall or at some other agreed-upon time during the year. Some congregations incorporate the distribution of recruitment forms within a service, as described earlier.

If you are facing resistance to incorporating a recruitment process into a worship service, don't give up. Instead, start small. I worked with a congregation's shared ministry team that, the first year, decided to ask if the recruitment forms could be handed out by ushers at the end of the service. The next year they received permission to put the forms in the pews and to receive a mention during the announcements. After a couple of years, leaders became open to the concept of a weekend centered on recruitment for ministry. They agreed to give the shared ministry director five minutes at the end of the homily to introduce members to the booklets in their pews and let them look through the choices and fill out a form.

Eventually a ministry member was allowed to give a two-minute talk about his experiences working in ministry, coupled with time to have members fill out their forms. Over time the pastor began to connect the homily to the invitation for all to serve. The music director began to select songs that spoke about sharing ones gifts and being part of the body of believers.

The shared ministry team, realizing that people did not have time to make good choices during the worship service, decided to mail copies of the ministry catalog several weeks prior to the recruitment event. This gave people time to look over the choices and make more thoughtful decisions about which ministries to sign up for.

As the years passed this whole process became a part of the faith community's culture and was carried out each fall on the weekend after Labor Day. It was put on the church's planning calendar as a matter of course. The concept of committing or recommitting to ministry became part of the annual cycle of events for this congregation.

This is what I mean by *building* the system of shared ministry. It doesn't happen overnight. The culture is changed gradually but persistently and deeply until it becomes a natural part of church life. The recruitment weekend becomes a way to make shared ministry come alive for the members of the congregation.

STEP 7: EVALUATE TRACKING SOFTWARE

The next step as you move toward recruitment is evaluating tracking tools available through your congregation's membership management software and other available software. Another reason it may take as long as a year to prepare for a churchwide recruitment is that preparing the tracking database can be a big job. Many congregations get nervous about this task. They worry about their lack of knowledge about good software design, the cost of having to purchase new software, and the question of who will support the software once installed.

Parish census software programs may contain components that track "activities." Some parishes have been able to adapt this activities category, changing the heading from "activities" to "ministries." One reason to make this change is to maintain consistent language as you are building the new culture. The word *activities* may be used to indicate such varied things as attendance at a retreat, participation in the congregation's baseball team, or membership in a Bible study group. Lumping these kinds of actions together with ministry involvement tends to adulterate the meaning of the word *ministry*.

You will first need to research the capabilities of your congregation's current software with the person who is most familiar with it. Your current software may already include the tracking capabilities you need. Increasingly, church-management software packages contain volunteer-management components. Stand-alone volunteer-management software packages are also available. Or your congregation's current software might have an add-on feature that will give you the needed capabilities. The cost of an add-on is usually much less than purchasing a new software package. One caveat—most "activities" categories do not offer enough fields to handle all a congregation's ministries and other important information you will need to keep track of. You need to find out if the number of these fields can be enlarged or if there is an upper limit.

You also will want to research other available commercial database programs. The cost of this type of software is fairly reasonable. You also gain the benefits of using a program likely familiar to most computer programmers. This will be valuable if you need assistance making changes to the program at a later date. Researching what other congregations are doing will help your shared ministry team make more informed decisions as well as shorten the learning curve.

Some of the larger software companies will offer free support and assistance with adding new fields to the database. They are often eager to create new components to their programs to add them to their products for future sales. If need be, you may want to point out to your software company how working with you to build a shared ministry database component would be of value to them. Essentially you are giving them a chance to do market research and design an element that they will be able to use in sales to other congregations. So it is to their advantage to work with you, a win-win situation for all. But the shared ministry director and team still need to be knowledgeable about what data and reports will be necessary. Few software companies have this specialized expertise.

A final alternative is to ask a congregation member, who is both knowledgeable and willing to spend the time, to create a custom database specifically designed to meet the needs of the shared ministry system. Whichever route you decide to use, it is very important that the designer works closely with a shared ministry representative to create a workable program.

Whether you decide to use software your congregation already owns, purchase a new program, or create a database of your own design, make sure that it can download members' names and addresses from software already in use, so that you will not have to re-enter all the information before you can begin to use the new software.

STEP 8: SELECT AND PREPARE THE CHOSEN SOFTWARE

To select and prepare the chosen software to receive data to be collected, you will want to think through carefully what data will be important to capture and what reports you will want. "Basic Components of a Shared Ministry Database," below, lists the information a shared ministry database should include, and "Shared Ministry Database Report Capabilities," on page 94, outlines reports and other features that shared ministry programs will find useful. These guides will help you evaluate whether a software package has all the capabilities you will need.

Basic Components of a Shared Ministry Database

- Log-in page
- Member information
  ○ Name
  ○ Birth date or age category: Child, youth, teen (ages 15 and up), adult
  ○ Address
  ○ City, state, zip code
  ○ Home phone, cell phone
  ○ Work phone
  ○ E-mail address
  ○ Unique identification number for each person (such as offering envelope number, church census database number, other ID number created by shared ministry database)
  ○ Unique identification code number for each ministry
- Ministries individual is involved in:

- ° Date sign-up information was received, whether new or recommitting to ministry, date follow-up contact was made, result of follow-up contact (yes—will definitely join ministry; no—will not join ministry at this time)
  ° Date ministry participation began
  ° Whether the person is a leader of this ministry
  ° Comment field to note volunteer ministers' special needs (for example, a handicapped-accessible work space), specific times available, or other unique information
- Ability to add or mark as inactive any ministry or category of ministries
- Ability to edit all personal information and ministry description information

Including age categories is useful for two reasons. First, it is very helpful to ministry leaders and staff members to know the age of the person who has submitted a recruitment form. Sometimes children fill out a form unsupervised and check off ministries intended for adults only. A staff person looking at the recruitment forms that have come in for ten new catechists might be surprised to find out that two of the ten are twelve-year-olds who are too young to serve in this position. Having this information on the form itself saves the staff person from making plans based on faulty information. Second, some congregations want to identify older teens, such as those over fifteen, to ensure volunteers have the maturity required to participate in certain ministries involving small children, such as nursery assistants, day camp counselors, and so forth.

Attaching an ID number to each volunteer minister avoids confusion when two people have the same name and makes it much easier to call up the individual and change or edit data in the computer record, handle situations where several members of one family are volunteering for different ministries, or keep track of an individual who changes his or her name or goes by several different names. The ID number also makes it easier to cross-reference

Request for Follow-Up

Staff Leader: Early, Amber **Work phone:** 654-555-4444

Ministry Leader: Good, Joseph **Home phone:** 651-555-0920

Category: FAI Faith Formation

Ministry: 135 Middle School Club Leader

Age Code	Person Name/ Address	Telephone/Email	Sign-up Date	Contact Date	Signup?	Comment
Adult/Yes	Trust, Mary 1234 Orange St Happy Valley, MN 55122	H-612-444-2344 maryt@email.com	09/18/2011			
Adult/No	Sweet, Roger 2345 Sunny St. New Prairie, MN 55146	Cell - 498-555-6666 H- 613-555-4432 rogers@email.com	09/18/2011			
Teen/No	Chandler, Marcie 999 Question St Happy Valley, MN 55122	H-612-555-9877	09/18/2011			

Figure 6.4. Ministry Summary Report, Request for Follow-up

Figure 6.4. Ministry Summary Report, Request for Follow-up

Report on Follow-Up Contacts

Category: CGG—Justice & Charity — Christian Giving　**Staff Leader:** Best, Stephanie　**Work phone:** 654-555-4444

Ministry: 13—Loaves and Fishes　**Ministry Leader:** Duty, Jeff　**Home phone:** 651-555-0920

Age Code/PBO	Person Name/ Address	Telephone/Email	Sign-up Date	Contact Date	Signup?	Comment
Adult	Jonson, John 1234 Apple St Happy Valley, MN 55122	H-612-555-5541 johnj@email.com	09/18/2011	10/15/2011	Yes	
Adult	Jonson, Judy 1234 Apple St Happy Valley, MN 55122	H-612-555-2278 judyj@email.com	09/18/2011	10/15/2001	Yes	
Teen	Jonway, Ben 1234 Berry St. Happy Valley, MN 55122	Cell-612-555-5556	09/20/2011	10/15/2011	No	New work schedule

Figure 6.5. Ministry Summary Report, after Follow-up

Figure 6.5. Ministry Summary Report, after Follow-up

an individual between two separate parts of the shared ministry database, such as between the ministry involvement section and the risk management section.

Figures 6.4 and 6.5 give examples of ministry summary reports for two different ministries. The first example, figure 6.4 shows a ministry summary report of people the ministry leader or recruiter needs to follow up on. Figure 6.5 shows a report that has been returned to the data entry administrator with information for the database after a follow-up contact has been made.

Shared Ministry Database Report Capabilities

A shared ministry database can generate the following types of reports and other resources:

- Ministries with their ministry code, ministry description, staff liaison, lay leader or coordinator, and organizational category
- Ministry participants' names and contact information, organized by general ministry category and specific ministry (for example, General Category: Faith Formation; Specific Ministry: Middle School Retreat Team), ministry code number.
- Mailing labels for a given ministry
- Individual's participation record in ministry, with all ministries person has been and is currently involved in, including ministry code, ministry name, sign-up date, contact date, start date, stop date, training date, flag for sending e-mail thank-you for signing up, date thank-you sent, flag for printing thank-you, date thank-you mailed
- Personal information for a given individual, including name, address, ID number, age or age category
- E-mail or hard copy thank-you letters
- All ministries in a specific category, such as all pastoral care ministries, with their codes, staff person, and lay leaders
- Total number of people involved in all ministries
- Number of people involved organized by age category, new or returning to ministry, sign-up date

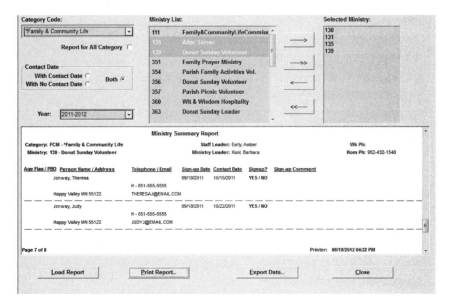

Figure 6.6 Ministry Summary Report

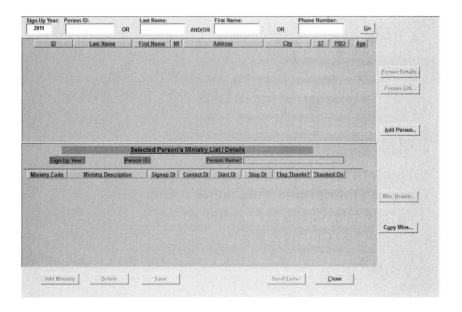

Figure 6.7 Blank Sign-up Screen

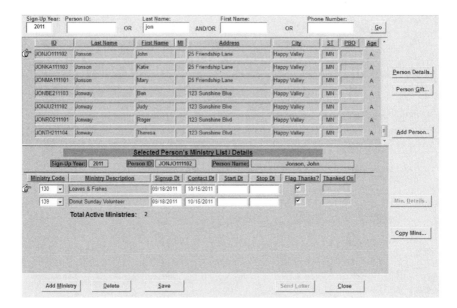

Figure 6.8 List of John Jonson's Ministries

- Total number of people engaged in a specific ministry or ministry category

The preceeding pages show screenshots from a shared ministry database. Figures 6.6, 6.7, and 6.8 include a ministry summary report, a blank sign-up screen, and a screen for locating people and linking them to ministries.[5]

Control of Information and Confidentiality

When you set up the shared ministry database, be prepared for initial objections from the person currently in charge of maintaining church membership data. Anyone with experience maintaining such a system will probably have nightmares about someone coming in and "mucking up the data" by making changes or not following procedures. Another serious concern is maintaining the confidentiality of data in the current system. Such concerns are entirely reasonable and understandable. It is very important to be sensitive to these fears and establish a good relationship with the person responsible for managing membership data.

If you are going to be using a part of the parish data system or a module that connects to it, the first thing to do is to establish passwords and protocols that will keep confidential information confidential. This should not be too difficult. Shared ministry database volunteers and leaders do not need to access an individual's financial records, counseling notes, or other confidential, personal information. They do need to access names, addresses, phone numbers, e-mail addresses, and birth dates for each individual. The most useful types of software allow downloading this information in some way.

I recommend that shared ministry information be accessible and maintained separately from the other membership data. Maintaining shared ministry data will ultimately become a large responsibility and require updating on a timely and ongoing basis. After an annual recruitment event, information needs to be recorded in the database very quickly so that names of new and returning ministry members may be distributed to leaders for follow-up. It will also be important to keep the information current and to be able to meet requests for reports in a timely manner. It generally does not work well to add such a time-sensitive task to a staff person's job.

I also strongly recommend that the director of shared ministry not be expected to keep this database updated. It can become an all-consuming job that will prevent the director from being able to work on other important components of the shared ministry system. Instead, make plans to create a new data-entry volunteer ministry, supervised by the director of shared ministry. This team can be of tremendous assistance in quickly entering data and preparing reports. The team will need to be recruited and trained before recruitment begins so that they can input information immediately. An alternative is to hire an administrative assistant for the director of shared ministry.

As data relating to shared ministry participation is accumulated, you can begin to reveal the success of the shared ministry recruitment system. The first year you do this, you will be establishing a baseline from which to measure growth of participation in ministry. Over time, you can compare numbers of people involved in a particular ministry or the retention rate of volunteer ministers from year to year. You can also tabulate how many people filled out recruitment forms from one year to the next. Such data is useful when congregation leaders want a picture of the progress and success of the shared ministry system. The director of shared ministry can also use this data in supervisory sessions with his or her own director.

STEP 9: DESIGN A FOLLOW-UP PROCESS

To ensure that people who fill out a sign-up form and turn it in will be contacted about their interest, you will need to design a follow-up process. One of the worst mistakes a congregation can make is to fail to follow up with an individual who has expressed interest in a ministry. Over and over I work with faith communities whose leaders tell me that they had a recruitment event of some sort with sign-up forms, but nobody ever followed up with the people who filled out the forms. Consequently, the system never caught hold and there is widespread cynicism whenever the suggestion is made to try it again. Several important processes can be put into place to ensure that the bad experience is not repeated.

Information Loops

A critical component to create in this recruitment process is what I call information loops. These are ways to make absolutely sure that information is passed quickly and accurately to all the parties needing it. When building these communication loops, the shared ministry team and staff person need to carefully think through who needs to know what and how the information can be passed between parties efficiently and quickly.

Personal Contact Information

You may have two databases operating independently of each other, which means that information entered into one may not be automatically shared with the other. What information loop can you build that will enable information to be shared smoothly and quickly between the two databases regardless of which database administrator first receives it? Creating this information loop between the shared ministry database and the congregation membership database will prevent discrepancies between the two databases, which waste time on attempts to find accurate information and money on mailings sent to incorrect addresses, and which lead to confused or missed communications.

Follow-up Processes

One important information loop includes the shared ministry database team, the leader of a particular ministry, and the staff liaison for that ministry, if there is one. When an individual signs up for a ministry, someone in the ministry needs to receive the information that a new person has signed up so that the person can be contacted and brought into the ministry. The shared ministry database team needs to send this information to the ministry head or recruiter as well as the staff person working with that area.

After a recruitment weekend, lists of people signing up for each ministry need to be sent out to all the ministry heads so they can follow up with the new volunteers. This can be done by e-mail, regular mail, pick-up boxes at church, or whatever effective method you devise. But the loop goes in two directions. A mechanism is needed for reporting back to the shared ministry database team that the new individual was indeed contacted and what the outcome of that contact was. This loop is key to preventing people from slipping through the cracks. It also ensures that shared ministry staff and team members know who is involved in each ministry. Merely filling out a form does not mean the individual has committed to joining a ministry, nor does a person's interest guarantee he or she has the gifts required for the ministry. This needs to be confirmed through personal contact by a representative of the particular ministry. The appropriate ministry leader should review the position description with those who are interested in serving to determine whether they understand the ministry and the responsibilities of the specific position, possess the needed gifts, can make an adequate time commitment, and so forth. Some positions might also require a background check before a person can participate.

Following Up on the Follow-up

Another information loop goes from the shared ministry database back to the director of shared ministry or another person who will "follow up on the follow-up" procedure. In other words, the system needs a mechanism that will flag people who were not contacted within an appropriate amount of time, so that they don't become one of those who are never contacted and as a result become disillusioned with the process. It will be much better to follow up with a ministry leader who is lagging behind in contacting potential new members than to deal with a disappointed potential volunteer minister who never was contacted.

STEP 10: BRIEF ALL LEADERS ABOUT THE PROCESS AND EXPECTATIONS

To have a successful recruitment campaign it is important to keep paid staff, pastors, and congregation and ministry leaders informed about what is going to happen and why and how they will be expected to participate. Therefore, you need to brief all congregation leaders, paid and volunteer, regarding the recruitment process and expectations for their participation. If you and your team have completed the preparations discussed to this point, these leaders will already know something about what you are trying to accomplish.

You will need the cooperation of ministry leaders and paid staff to do the following:

- Promote the ideals of shared ministry to their committees.
- Write a brief description of their ministries for the recruitment brochure.
- Write or edit position descriptions for each ministry.
- Agree to fully participate in the recruitment weekend and follow-up schedule during what is possibly a very hectic time for them.
- Follow up *promptly* with all people who sign up for their ministries or assign someone else to do so.
- Keep the members of their ministries informed about the recruitment process, schedule, and expectations.
- Work hard to meet deadlines for completing brief ministry descriptions, position descriptions, and contacting potential new members.
- Encourage current ministry members to fill out a sign-up form so that the database will contain reliable information.

The above list should make it apparent that the cooperation and participation of ministry leaders is essential to the ultimate success of a recruitment event.

STEP 11: PUBLICIZE THE RECRUITMENT EVENT

Because of its behind-the-scenes nature, shared ministry tends to be a well-kept secret unless you make determined efforts to educate members about the goals and values of this new culture. The recruitment event offers a perfect time to introduce the community at large to the concept of shared ministry and to publicize the formation of a shared ministry team.

The recruitment weekend should be well publicized as it approaches. Procedures for obtaining position descriptions and signing up for ministries, the follow-up process, and other details need to be explained. Use as many vehicles as possible to get the word out, including newsletters, worship bulletins, announcements during worship, an information booth before and after weekend services, the congregation's website, parish-wide e-mails, bulletin boards, videos, church blogs, Twitter, and so forth.

STEP 12: RECRUIT AND TRAIN DATA-ENTRY VOLUNTEERS

Once the database is up and running, recruit and train people to input data from the returned recruitment forms. This is an opportunity to connect with members who may have never participated in ministry before. Look for those with experience with data entry, who are comfortable working by themselves, and who have gifts of attention to detail and fast typing skills. You will want to create a training model and schedule so that the data entry team will be well prepared to begin as soon as the recruitment event has concluded. It is wise to arrange for someone knowledgeable about the database to be available the first time each data-entry person works on this to answer questions, review processes, and offer other support.

Ongoing Recruitment Methods

Up to now I have been talking about efforts to create a single congregation-wide recruitment event. While this is a key component of the shared ministry system, it does not cover all the recruitment requirements and opportunities.

Some areas of ministry are cyclical in nature. Religious education classes for children and teens, Habitat for Humanity ministries, parish festivals, and the like come to mind. Key recruitment times for these ministries may not coincide with the annual recruitment weekend event discussed above. For example, an annual fall recruitment drive may occur too late for the religious education ministries to obtain the number of volunteer ministers they need to teach their classes. Some congregations recruit ministry members at the same time as they register students for classes. Others run a mini-recruitment drive for the fall semester in late spring. Habitat for Humanity groups may hold special recruitments before each new building project begins. More sophisticated ministries may have a yearlong plan for recruiting members in various ways.

The shared ministry director and team need to be flexible and sensitive to the needs of ministries to hold their own specific recruitment events at times different from the annual recruitment event. The fact that your congregation has an annual recruitment event should not preclude other efforts. However, it is important to include those seasonal ministry opportunities in your annual recruitment booklet to maintain the all-inclusive nature of the event. A few people will sign up during the congregation-wide event, and they can be used as backups, substitutes, and assistants to the majority of volunteer ministers recruited through drives focused on specific ministries. This is part of the unified system you are building. The shared ministry director and team can act as resource people to ministries as they plan their own recruitment events. Support and encouragement for these seasonal ministries will ensure that including all ministries in the main event will be an accepted process and not seen as a needless duplication of effort. While their own focused recruitment efforts will no doubt provide these ministries with most of their volunteer ministers, the annual congregation-wide event can provide additional people and publicity for the needs of these ministries.

As the congregation's culture changes over time, the process of an annual recruitment event becomes a standard part of the congregation's life. All members understand that they need to fill out a recruitment form annually, regardless of whether they are new or returning to a given ministry. Everyone who fills out a recruitment form also expects to be promptly contacted.

In addition, no shame or guilt is attached to a volunteer minister deciding to move to a different ministry or even to take some time out to rest, handle family issues, or deal with the demands of work. The annual recruitment is seen as a perfect time to make these changes. Ministries collaborate with the shared ministry team by providing accurate information for the yearly recruitment booklet. Paid staff and ministry leaders follow up with both new and returning ministry members as soon as possible, using lists generated by the shared ministry database. Ministry leaders provide updated information to the shared ministry database in a timely fashion.

Remember, these changes will only come about gradually. Some people will never get it. But a majority of the membership will be on board, as explained in the preceding paragraph. Remember also that culture change doesn't just happen. It requires dedication and persistence in building all the components. Patience is the watchword. Trust in the power of God's grace is essential.

CHAPTER 7

Celebrating Ministry, Expressing Gratitude

Many times lack of support is a key reason churches have trouble retaining volunteer ministers after they are recruited. The word *support* encompasses a wide range of activities that help the ministers to do their work well, to feel appreciated, and to experience personal growth while using their gifts in an effective way. When congregations lack a comprehensive system for providing support, the faith community may be deprived of people's gifts. Some ministry members will drop out. Others will never volunteer in the first place, because they perceive that the elements of support important for them are missing. A prospective volunteer may learn, for example, that there is no orientation to the ministry work and shy away from volunteering because he feels ill-equipped to carry out the work without such an orientation. Because this book is about getting started in building a shared ministry system, I will concentrate on just one area of support that is important to most volunteer ministers—experiencing gratitude for the unique efforts each person brings to his or her ministry.

Many faith communities expect the particular ministry leader and the ministry area to say thank you to their own volunteer ministers. However, without a comprehensive system in place, many ministries might not express appreciation. The reasons are many. Ministry leaders might not participate because they lack the time, fail to understand the importance of this element in supporting volunteer ministers, or are unaware that in a shared ministry culture, there is an expectation that each ministry show individualized appreciation. The director of shared ministry and team need to (1) encourage and support the efforts of each ministry that does have a method for expressing appreciation for each of its members, and (2) urge those ministries that don't have any such process in place to create one. As needed, they can act as resources to the various ministry groups, suggesting ways to accomplish individualized appreciation. This area of support, which I call expressing gratitude, can take three forms: affirmation, appreciation, and celebration. Figure 7.1 outlines the differences among the processes.

Affirmation	Appreciation	Celebration
Personal	Personal	Communal
Confirming the worth of the individual	Expressing thanks for participating in a specific ministry	Rejoicing in accomplishments of the ministries as a whole
Valuing presence	Recognizing a job well done	Participating as a community
Valuing individual uniqueness	Praising successful use of gifts	Recognizing official and unofficial ministry efforts
Ongoing throughout experience	Specific, individualized, timely	Generalized, broadly inclusive, periodic

Figure 7.1. Comparison of Affirmation, Appreciation, and Celebration

An example of *affirmation* would be saying to a minister, "Hi! So glad you are here today. How are you doing after your foot surgery?" An example of *appreciation* might be writing a note thanking the volunteer minister for her recent participation and mentioning how her special gifts contributed to the effort: "Without your able leadership at our team meetings, keeping us on track and summarizing discussions so well, we would never have been able to accomplish our project within the allotted time frame." *Celebration* refers to a congregation-wide event rejoicing in the work and worth of all the ministries, and volunteers within those ministries, as a whole. It may also involve recognizing the many unofficial ways people minister in their families, communities, places of work, and schools. A celebration event thanks worshipers and financial supporters for their important contributions to the mission of the church as well. All three of these processes are important to instill in the life of the congregation as the shared ministry system is built. When addressing the area of support, I advise concentrating on these processes first.

Affirmation is important because it recognizes the person for *who they are*. Our Christian faith teaches us that all individuals have worth because they are created by God. Our recognition of ministers goes beyond the work they can contribute to the group. They have value to us just because they are who they are. This aspect is central to a shared ministry approach.

Appreciation is a familiar experience for most individuals. In everyday life people are accustomed to thanking others and to being thanked. It is one of those social expectations that makes human interactions go more smoothly. On that basis alone people expect that someone will express thanks for their efforts in ministry. Even though most people will say that they are not working in the ministry in order to be thanked, nevertheless everyone has a psychological need to feel their efforts are appreciated.

Celebration recognizes the ministry that goes on throughout the congregation. It is important because it joins the individual's work in a particular ministry to the mission of the entire faith community. It raises awareness in the congregation as a whole of the many ways people are contributing to that mission. It says that the ministry of the congregation is carried out by all members, whether or not they are currently engaged in a specific ministry themselves. Celebrations are a unifying force within the faith community. A celebration event is also an opportunity for the shared ministry team to once again promote the system in a concrete way.

As the shared ministry director and team work to ensure that leaders of each ministry are expressing appreciation to their own individual members, they first need to reflect on the traditions of their congregation. Compile as much information as you can on the types of ministry celebration and appreciation that currently exist, rather than assuming that nothing like this is being done in the congregation. Are there ministries or clusters of ministries doing such events on a regular basis? Some ministries already have a tradition for saying thank you to individual members. Faith formation classes and teen ministries are two areas where you are likely to find established ways for thanking teachers and helpers. Some ministry teams host an annual picnic, potluck, or other such event. Larger ministries may send out thank-you cards or give their members token gifts each year. You don't want to undo or negate what is already in place and working well. Of course, shared ministry leaders will also want to determine which ministries have no such process in place.

It is important to identify the leaders who need to be included in planning any changes to tradition. While it is definitely a part of the shared ministry team's responsibility to make sure each ministry expresses some kind of appreciation to its members at an appropriate time, the team has to be sensitive to what has gone on before and tread lightly in suggesting any changes. It is best to include all stakeholders in the discussions when a change is being considered.

A Celebration of Ministry

For some congregations, the shared ministry director, committee, staff, and lay leaders may determine that creating a system-wide celebration event is the most pressing need. The need may be especially great for those faith communities that have not had any general tradition of thanking ministry members or for those experiencing widespread burnout among ministry members. When planning strategically for an effective way to introduce shared ministry to the congregation, other considerations contribute to making the decision to do an appreciation event before the recruitment event. These considerations may be logistical, such as time of year when the shared ministry committee can most easily plan and present such an event, where the church is in its annual cycle of seasons and programs, or how important the need is to church leaders. Strategically, this kind of event may be put together faster and more easily than a full recruitment drive.

The purpose of the event is to provide a way for the entire faith community to celebrate and appreciate all the congregation's ministries. Many faith communities plan an event for all volunteer ministers, such as a dinner or brunch, at which representative leaders express a general thank-you and provide food, fellowship, and possibly entertainment. To prepare, however, the planning committee needs to do its homework in a couple of areas.

As noted above, great care should be taken to ensure that longstanding traditions are not co-opted without the full understanding and cooperation of the ministry areas involved. Can the practices of ministries be somehow woven into the big plan? Or can the particular ministry be persuaded to try this new method for celebrating its members' work? Any ministries or staff members who have already established ways to thank the members they work with need to be reassured that this churchwide celebration of ministry will not supplant their own. Rather, encourage these ministries to participate in both their traditional way and in this parish-wide celebration. The shared ministry committee and director need to communicate that the big event is something that everyone participates in. It celebrates all the gifts of the congregation and the work of all in advancing the mission. But this does not mean that individual ministries cannot or should not maintain their unique traditions as well.

Another task for the shared ministry committee and director is to look at what types of churchwide events bring out the most people. Do lots of people seem to enjoy a brunch after Sunday services? Do you get a lot of participation at any other community events such as church dinners, picnics, ice cream socials, or parish dances? Which are better attended: weekday evening or weekend events? If something is already working for you, by all means go in that direction.

Unfortunately, the trend seems to be that drawing a crowd for these kinds of events is becoming more difficult. The typical volunteer luncheon, appreciation dinner, brunch, or similar event can be a disappointment to the organizers, who have put much time and energy into planning the event only to have it attended by a minority of the volunteer ministers. If the attendance at such functions has historically been sparse, then the committee has several choices. One is to look for creative ways to build events into times when people are already likely to be at church. Weaving in a ministry celebration time during weekend services may ensure the highest level of participation. It holds up to all those attending, even those who may not be currently involved in shared ministry, the value the congregation places on volunteer ministry in general.

Many congregations have had great success developing a theme for their celebrations. The theme might be tied to the season of the church year or the calendar year:

- The feast of Pentecost: "We celebrate the gifts of the Spirit, given to us for mission."
- The Advent season: "We share our gifts—skills, passions, time, and experience—with the faith community."
- Annual stewardship emphasis: "We recognize members' stewardship of their gifts of service."
- Discipleship themes: "We celebrate our discipleship lived out in ministry."
- A fall harvest of gifts or Thanksgiving theme: "We celebrate with thankful praise the gifts for ministry God has bestowed on us."
- Mardi Gras: "We celebrate the gifts of all our members over the past year that move us toward fulfillment of our mission as a community of faith."

- Individual sermons or a series relating to the gifts of all the volunteer ministers in the church: "Each of us is gifted by God for service."
- Spring celebration of gifts: "New life springs forth! See the gifts growing in our congregation."

The possibilities are many. My recommendation is that such an event be cast as a celebration in which all members can participate, rather than focusing only on those involved in the official ministries of the church. It is counterproductive to make some members feel excluded or of less worth because they are not now working in ministry. An upbeat, appreciative, and inviting atmosphere will go far toward opening the way for participating in ministry in the future. Remember that everything you do in shared ministry will affect all parts of the system, including future recruitment and retention.

The shared ministry team and the director need to be careful not to make the assumption, or imply to the parish, that the only "real" ministry or the only "valuable" ministry occurs within the walls of the church and is a part of the official established ministries of the congregation. Many people are doing wonderful, Spirit-led ministry out in their communities, places of work, schools, and families. The members who come faithfully to worship and those who contribute out of their financial means are doing ministry as well, through their support of the work of the church. What might this celebration look like?

One congregation has a tradition of celebrating ministry on the last weekend prior to the start of the season of Lent. The decorations in the gathering space and social hall reflect a different theme each year relating to celebrating the gifts offered through ministry participation. During worship, special banners are carried in the opening procession and arranged in the sanctuary. Hymns and music are chosen to reflect the theme. The pastor asks all present to celebrate the ministry that is performed and the gifts of time, skill, interest, and passion that are given to the faith community throughout the year. For the recessional, the congregation's musicians are joined by professionals hired just for the day as they play a joyful song to close the liturgy. The choir leads the congregation to the social hall to hear the professional musicians present a half hour of music from a particular musical genre. One year the music may be salsa, another year Dixieland, another year blues, rock and roll, and so forth. Instead of serving the usual donuts and coffee, organizers provide special foods, such as bagels and cream cheese, flavored coffees, or foods celebrating the ethnicities of church members. Appreciation buttons are personalized on the spot for all who desire one. Coloring sheets and word games are placed on the tables to occupy children. The idea is "God has blessed us. We rejoice as a community in appreciation of each other's contributions, all gifts from a gracious God."

Another congregation tied its celebration event to the liturgical day of Pentecost, which marks the time when God sent the Holy Spirit to the apostles after Jesus ascended into heaven. This congregation also scheduled its event during weekend services, to ensure the highest participation. Hundreds of tongues of fire were painted on cardboard and suspended from the ceiling of the worship space. As people arrived they were given a lapel pin with a message about celebrating the gifts God had given them. The selected music focused on the gifts of the Spirit and inviting people to use them in ministry. The pastor's sermon centered on celebrating all the gifts of God's people. Special prayers were offered in thanksgiving for each of the ministry areas in the church, such as liturgical, educational, and pastoral care ministries. Several volunteer ministers gave short talks about their experiences using their gifts in ministry. They shared what they had gained from the process. An outdoor ice cream social, to which the entire congregation was invited, followed the weekend services.

The design of the celebration will depend on the size of the congregation, the available budget, and how many volunteer ministers have attended past events. Other parishes have had a tradition of the paid staff planning and hosting a celebration specifically intended for all the volunteer ministers in the church. I know of one congregation that goes all out, with skits put on by the paid staff, live music, catered appetizers, and so forth. Sometimes paid staff gets completely burned out on this responsibility, because they have to devote precious time to all the planning and preparation that are necessary to make this kind of event happen. The paid staff may welcome a different format and having the shared ministry committee participate in the planning and preparation. But it is entirely appropriate for staff to participate in the celebration event in a very visible way. After all, the volunteer ministers are making it possible for the staff to do their work in helping the congregation reach its goals and objectives. Pastors and paid staff need to be actively present at these appreciation events.

In larger churches it will not be possible for a congregational event to be carried out only by the shared ministry team and staff. Other ministry volunteers will have to assist. Primary responsibility for a celebration of ministries lies with the shared ministry team, however. It acts in a servant capacity to the rest of the congregation. Its role is to assist in planning and executing the celebration event. The director of shared ministry may thank team members for their overall service in shared ministry at a separate event, but every effort should be made soon after the event to in some way thank everyone assisting in the celebration.

This community-wide attention to the ministry of the body of believers is a key aspect of a shared ministry congregation. It will be one of the important ways the culture of shared ministry begins to be formed. It also demonstrates in a visible and concrete way what the shared ministry team and director are about.

Appreciating Individuals or Groups of Ministers

The congregation-wide celebration of ministry is one important element in the life of the congregation. But it is generally not sufficient to meet people's need to feel they are recognized and appreciated for their efforts as individuals. Personalized appreciation is equally important.

Expressions of thanks need not be elaborate to be meaningful. For example, in some smaller committees and teams, the leader sends members thank-you notes acknowledging the specific contributions each individual has made to the work of that ministry. Studies in the nonprofit volunteer world have shown over and over again that people most like to be thanked with a personal, handwritten note. Yes, even in this age of e-mail and texting, people overwhelmingly prefer a personal note from someone who has worked with them or knows firsthand what their contribution has been.

The shared ministry director or team members might suggest this practice for leaders of other teams who are thinking about ways to say thank you. For ministries with large numbers of participants, it may make sense for key lay leaders in the ministry to assist the staff person or ministry head in writing these notes. Leaders of various subgroups, coordinators, schedulers, and the like can take responsibility for writing thank-you notes for the members of their group. For example, the lead usher at a particular weekend service could write notes for the ushers at that service. Age-level coordinators could write thank-you notes for all the teachers in their age group.

Similarly, teachers can be urged to write a note of appreciation for their assistant teachers, parent helpers, or coleaders. Staff members can write such notes for the leaders of the ministries with whom they work. The pastor can write notes to his or her governing council or committee and the paid staff. Some churches offer several preprinted versions of a general thank-you note that can be personalized with just a line or two to the particular person and be signed by a leader. Smaller congregations will be able to personally thank ministry members much more easily than large ones.

Whether large or small, some congregations may face a challenge in mailing thank-you notes. One congregation's solution was to couple a process of individualized personal appreciation methods with the churchwide celebration discussed above. They placed, tables throughout the social area with handwritten, personalized thank-you notes addressed to each member of the particular ministry. During the socializing time, volunteer ministers could make the rounds and collect their own thank-you notes from these tables, which were staffed by the ministry leaders or paid staff. At the time an individual came to a particular ministry table, the staff person or lay leader would thank the person verbally as well. While perhaps not an ideal situation, this process illustrates how congregations may need to make compromises as they work toward more effective solutions. With the advent of Internet technology, other solutions are possible, such as sending thank-you notes to individuals via e-mail.

EXAMPLES OF THANK-YOU NOTES

Example 1: To a Ministry Leader

Dear Tom,

I would like to thank you for your leadership of our New Fathers' Support Group this past year. We had an average attendance of thirty-five men (75 percent of the new dads in our congregation) at our monthly sessions. Evaluations consistently praised the relevance of the topics presented.

Your organizational skills in locating appropriate speakers, recruiting small group leaders, and arranging for refreshments at each meeting made it possible for participants in this group to gain good parenting skills while enjoying fellowship with other men experiencing parenthood for the first time.

Because of your energy and ability to see our vision and impart it to others, you contributed to our church's mission of outreach to young families in our community. Thanks again, and I look forward to working with you next year, if you are able to continue in this leadership position.

Sincerely,

Bob Smith
Family Life Coordinator

Example 2: To a Ministry Member

Dear Betty,

Thanks for being part of our food-shelf restocking team this year. I appreciated your dependability. I knew I could always rely on you coming in on your scheduled day. It was also so helpful that you were willing to put in extra hours when we were especially busy. Because of your cheerful availability, I was able to entrust the work of this ministry to you at times when my attention was required elsewhere. Thanks for being such a great ministry partner. I hope to see you back here next fall.

Sincerely,

Mary Nichols, Director
Ministries of Charity and Support

If the particular ministry is very large or participants are somewhat anonymous in the way they perform their work (for example, a large number of people contribute regularly to the food shelf), it may be logistically impossible to write personalized notes to hundreds of people. The next best thing may be a postcard or note that acknowledges the accomplishments of the ministry as a whole. For example, "Because of your generous donations, our food shelf was able to serve forty-nine families this year with supplementary food." Or, "Your donation to our Christmas mitten and scarf tree allowed us to distribute 150 scarves and 200 pairs of mittens to homeless shelters and women's safe houses." A short handwritten message or at least the ministry leader's handwritten signature may be included at the bottom.

Another alternative is to hand out a token gift the next time the volunteer ministers participate in the ministry. The acknowledgment might be as simple as a thank-you card and an apple given to people as they drop off their donations. Even the fact that another human being shows this gesture of appreciation makes it meaningful to the receiver. This personalized appreciation can be offered at the same time of year as the parish-wide ministry celebration event or at the conclusion of a task or ministry cycle. For example the Christmas mitten and scarf collectors could receive thank-you notes shortly after the start of the New Year. Habitat for Humanity volunteers could be thanked at the conclusion of their work. A congregation's board members might gather for an annual appreciation dinner after the Christmas and New Year's holidays.

Affirmation

Affirmation recognizes the individual for who he or she is, for being a person in ministry regardless of what he or she does, for participating in the life of the faith community.

In some ways this is almost more difficult to do than a thank-you note or celebration event, because it requires getting to know people as individuals and recognizing their presence in small ways *throughout the course of their service.* Some examples are greeting the individual when she arrives for her ministry work; listening thoughtfully during conversations; making a point of observing his work and offering feedback; sharing an article; asking about the family, the job, the kids, the parents; calling and asking about her ministry experience; having a meal or coffee together; calling the volunteer and expressing concern when he is absent; and inviting the minister to serve as a mentor or trainer. These seemingly little actions let individuals know that their presence is appreciated, that they are important children of God. They say to the minister, "You are an important part of this church. We are glad you are here."

The larger the ministry the more difficult it becomes to provide such individual attention. However, affirmation need not come only from a paid staff member. The lay leader of the ministry, shared ministry team members, members of the board, the pastor, the maintenance person mopping the floor—each one can make it a point to connect with people as individuals at every opportunity. In fact, a congregation that has an established culture of shared ministry should see this kind of affirmation going on at all levels of the organization, with ministers affirming each other, staff affirming other staff, and so forth.

These three aspects of support—celebration, appreciation, and affirmation—are crucial in keeping a vibrant ministry life going in the church and an integral part of creating the culture of shared ministry in your church.

CHAPTER 8

Keeping Everybody Safe

A vital component of any shared ministry system is protecting those being served, the volunteer ministers providing the service, and the congregation itself from harm. The term *risk management* is often applied to the policies and procedures put in place to make the church environment as safe as possible. This term can be used to refer to a wide spectrum of activities designed to minimize risk in many different areas, such as legal liability, health and safety, buildings and grounds, and employment practices.

There are many kinds of abuse, including physical, such as a teacher physically punishing children, and emotional, such as a supervisor who constantly demeans a staff member through humiliating comments. Vulnerable elders may suffer abuse if their financial resources are appropriated by unscrupulous relatives or caretakers. In this chapter, I will focus on ways to protect the vulnerable people churches serve from sexual abuse. There are several reasons for this particular focus: Sexual abuse is more prevalent in church settings than other kinds of abuse. It is difficult to discover, given the element of threat by perpetrators, the powerlessness of victims, and its secretive nature. Sexual abuse is a life-changing event for an individual. Its ramifications extend into the family, congregation, community, and denomination levels.

This is an area for which volunteer ministers need to be pre-screened, educated about policies and procedures, and effectively supervised. Even for those who are just starting to build a shared ministry culture, and as complex as dealing with this topic is, protecting people from sexual abuse has to be a priority for the director, shared ministry team, and faith community. My recommendations are the result of both my study and my practical experience as a director of shared ministry. However, each congregation has a responsibility to find out the legal requirements for the congregation based on its state and local statutes, insurance coverage, and denominational rules. Shockingly, the sexual abuse of minors and vulnerable adults appears to be endemic in many church cultures. However, the absence of known sexual abuse in a congregation is no assurance that past instances may not be discovered or that it will not occur in the future.

The news media bombard us almost weekly with reports about sexual abuse cases, whether they occurred in the recent past or many years ago. One of the reasons this topic never grows old is that its effects are so devastating and can disturb its victims throughout their lives. Sexual abuse is not something that the individual can just get over or put behind her or him. It causes problems for the victims in every significant area of their lives, damaging their sense of trust, social and family interactions, personality, sense of self-worth, and relationship with God and the church, not to mention their sexual identity and ability to have a loving, self-giving relationship with a life partner.

Anyone involved in building a shared ministry culture has a duty to do everything possible to protect the vulnerable of any age from suffering this devastation. We also have a duty to protect our volunteer ministers from unwittingly getting into situations in which their actions can be misinterpreted or that put them at risk of allegations of abuse that are not true. False allegations can be devastating for the accused and innocent providers of ministry to children and vulnerable adults. If your parish has no risk management policies and procedures in place, this must be one of your top priorities in building a shared ministry system. It is an ethical, moral imperative. Many denominations require their member churches to do background checks, ensure a certain number of adults are present at all youth and children classes and events, and so on. You will want to investigate your denomination's rules or guidelines as well as those that may already be in place for your congregation.

Getting Everybody on Board

If your congregation has no official policy and procedures, you may first need to persuade the main decision makers and leaders that the congregation must seriously look at this important aspect of ministry. Denial is simply not an option. If your parish is one in which key leaders are still in denial about the need for such policies and procedures, you will need to work diligently to change their attitudes. In the book *No Surprises: Controlling Risk in Volunteer Programs,* authors Charles Tremper and Gwynne Kostin state, "Denial substitutes deliberate ignorance for thoughtful planning."[1] Ignorance is not a legal defense in the event of an abuse case originating in your congregation.

Gather a group of concerned, knowledgeable members to put together a rationale for facing this topic. Good people to recruit are social workers, pediatricians, lawyers and judges who work with family and abuse issues, nurses, and teachers. Anyone who is an adult volunteer with a youth organization that has strict rules about adult screenings, such as the Boy Scouts, the Girl Scouts, youth mentoring organizations, and so forth could be another helpful member of this group. Also look for corporate human resources people, directors of volunteers, experienced volunteers who work in other nonprofit organizations, church staff or unpaid leaders who work with children and vulnerable adults, concerned parents, and people who have an interest in and gifts for writing policies. If some of these people hold leadership positions in your congregation, so much the better. You will have more clout and more easily get the attention of the rest of the leadership.

An excellent resource is the book *Reducing the Risk II: Making Your Church Safe from Child Sexual Abuse* by James F. Cobble Jr.,

Richard R. Hammar, and Steven W. Klipowicz.[2] It provides convincing arguments and statistics to persuade church leadership to seriously address the issue. It includes videos, class outlines, and lots of other tools helpful in building a risk management system.

Because of the magnitude of this topic and the amount of time and number of resources that will be required to deal with it, you will want to recruit a risk management team devoted to this shared ministry component alone. Team members could be drawn from the same people you recruited to help convince church leaders about the necessity of designing policies and procedures guarding against sexual abuse. However, some people may be interested only in getting approval for starting a risk management program, not in participating on a team with ongoing responsibilities. Regardless of the size of the congregation, recruiting such a team permits you to tap into experiences and gifts that members of the shared ministry team may not possess. It increases the number of people becoming involved in designing shared ministry policies and procedures, and the likelihood of getting support for the process from more members. Because you will be ultimately designing policies and procedures that will affect many of the ministries in your congregation, it is expedient to include some key ministry leaders on your team. You want to ensure that there will be majority buy-in by all concerned.

Dealing with risk management issues is a two-pronged process. One prong consists of clear policies about what behaviors will and will not be tolerated in your congregation. The policies are meant to stand for some time and to be general rules for the staff and members. Changing a policy requires going through specific formal processes.

The other prong is procedures. Procedures are specific operating actions designed to make the policy a reality. They can quickly be adapted to changing circumstances, as deemed acceptable by the leadership team. It is not necessary to go through formal approval processes to change procedures. Procedures assure that all ministries are conforming to the policies. They spell out exactly how people will implement the policies. These would include such things as screening requirements, such as interviewing and background checks; training requirements; supervision practices; reporting tools, such as incident reports; and how data will be collected and used to keep track of important information, such as the results from background checks. Other examples of procedures could include putting windows in all classroom doors, ensuring two adults are present with every group of children, and developing drop-off and pick-up processes for children in the nursery.

Procedures are not written into policies. They can, therefore, more easily be adapted to meet needs and new information as these arise. For example, say that you have adopted a *policy* that all members of ministries dealing with children and vulnerable adults must have a background check done by XYZ company before beginning their ministry work. As technology continues to evolve, more effective and efficient ways of accomplishing this same process could be developed. Or company XYZ might go out of business. Or you might simply find another company that does a more thorough job for a lower price. If this requirement has been written into a *policy*, as above, you will need to go through official channels to change and approve the policy before instituting the new process. If the matter is dealt with as a *procedure*, it can be more quickly and easily adapted to fit changing knowledge and needs, with possibly just a yearly update to your council indicating how the policy is being fulfilled.

If there are few or no risk management policies and procedures in place in your congregation, the best way to start is to examine the entire ministry framework from top to bottom for potential risk situations. The following list of "Risk Management Basics" outlines the process. Note that the first three items on this list provide you with an overall picture of what each ministry does and where the risks are likely to be. Once you have this information, you can create procedures that will minimize the identified risks. Identifying potential risks and risky ministries can provide background for writing the actual policy as well. Because procedures are very specific and policies are general, work on both processes can occur simultaneously.

Risk Management Basics

1. Assess the risks, looking at all your ministry areas in detail. What are the risks inherent in each ministry?
2. Determine which ministries carry the highest risk, assessing them according to some scale or other tool such as figures 8.1 and 8.2 on pages 127 and 129.
3. Choose a method of control or a way to lower the threat of potential risks.
4. Research and create a policy. Take it through the official approval processes for your congregation.
5. Put the policy into effect and ensure compliance.
6. Create operating procedures for all high-risk areas.
7. Develop position descriptions.
8. Publicize the risk management policy.
9. Regularly review and revise the policies and procedures.

ASSESS THE RISKS

Who is at risk? Look for situations in which opportunities for sexual abuse could arise. Investigate your ministries one by one. Analyze carefully what could go wrong at every step as the ministry is performed. This will involve talking with other staff members and volunteers about exactly how things work in the various ministry areas.

In one large parish, children's ministry leaders took fifty to seventy-five children, ages five to nine, out of each church service on Sunday and led them to the fellowship hall. There the leaders presented the appointed Scripture readings in language the children could understand and conducted a short discussion and prayer before returning the children to their families in the main worship space. The director of shared ministry met with the ministry leaders to determine whether children could be at risk during their time away from their parents. The ministry already required a minimum of two adults to work with each group of children. However, when the two leaders led the group of youngsters out of the church, they usually walked through busy halls filled with many people, most of whom no one in the ministry knew.

Occasionally several children would take a detour into the bathrooms. Because no adult was bringing up the rear of the group, the leaders usually did not notice that they had "lost" one or two children. In the discussion, it became apparent that in such a large parish, any stranger could pick up one of the stragglers and carry the child off with no one being the wiser. So the shared ministry director and children's ministry leaders decided that one adult would always walk behind the group to ensure no child left the line in transit. If the people working on procedures had not had a thorough discussion with those ministry leaders about exactly what went on in that ministry, the potential danger to children would probably never have been noticed until something happened.

Having conversations about potential risks also provides a wonderful opportunity to gain staff members' and lay leaders' interest and cooperation in the risk management process. When it becomes apparent that you have the best interests of the vulnerable at heart, this assurance often engenders trust and a willingness to make needed changes. As part of this evaluation of possible risk, compare the written (and unwritten) expectations for volunteers with their ability to perform the tasks they are assigned. Look at position descriptions. Are there any? Potential risk can occur when there are discrepancies between what a position description says and what is actually expected on the job. For example, a position description for middle-school helpers in the church nursery could state, "Help supervise children's play." Upon investigation the director of shared ministry learns that the middle-school students are expected to take toddlers to the bathroom alone and assist them with all their needs there. This is a significant expectation, but it is not written into the position description. The only way to discover this discrepancy is by having a conversation with middle-school students, the lay coordinator, the staff person in charge of the nursery, or all three to learn exactly what actions the students perform in the course of helping with the ministry. After identifying a potential risk, steps can be taken to minimize it. In this example, these steps might mean including the bathroom duties in the position description and making sure all helpers receive thorough training on the correct procedures for taking toddlers to the bathroom; keeping bathroom doors open at all times; having an adult always accompany the middle-school student and toddler; prohibiting the young teens from doing this particular task; and so forth.

DETERMINE RISK LEVELS

Identify the ministries and situations in which the possibility of serious harm occurring is highest.

To make effective use of their time, the risk management team will need to determine which ministries should receive attention first. This is especially true for congregations that have no risk management policies to start with. For example, a lower priority might be given to a ministry that brings snacks for children during their educational events, while developing procedures for one in which adults accompany teens on an overnight retreat would be a high priority.

Because the overnight retreat has a potentially higher risk for sexual abuse to occur, the team will want to make sure there is a position description for this ministry, that any required screening processes are spelled out and completed for each volunteer minister, that results of screenings are documented, and that any required trainings for the adults are developed and presented prior to an overnight. That is a lot of ground to cover for just one

Volunteer Position Title: _____

Ministry Area: _____

- Age and maturity of ministry recipient versus age and maturity of ministry provider
- Amount of time ministry provider spends with recipient per session: Minutes? Hours? Days?
- Frequency of involvement between provider and recipient: One time only? Weekly? Monthly?
- Length of involvement over time between provider and recipient: For a single day? Several days, weeks, months? For a year?
- Level of exclusivity: One-on-one? Private setting? Public group activity? Small group? Large group?
- Nature of relationship between recipient and provider of service: Counseling? Teaching? Chaperoning? Mentoring? Providing other service, such as driving the recipient to the store, cleaning house, yard work, and so forth? Facilitating a support group? Home visitor?
- Type of supervision provided: Supervision could occur directly between the supervisor and the minister. Are the recipient and provider always within the view of the supervisor? Is there a check-in with the supervisor during each volunteer episode? Supervision could be indirect. Does the volunteer minister send a written report to the supervisor? Does he or she check in by phone periodically? Are there periodic peer discussion sessions with the supervisor?
- Frequency of supervision: Weekly? Monthly? Sporadically? No supervision?

Figure 8.1. Assessing Ministry Risk: Points to Consider

ministry. Yet it is important to make sure all the bases are covered prior to an event. This involves either the director of shared ministry or a risk management team member meeting with the staff member and lay leaders of the ministry, obtaining their cooperation, and planning with them how best to complete these requirements.

Figures 8.1 and 8.2 are examples of ways to evaluate ministries according to the level of risk they represent to children and vulnerable adults. The first list, "Assessing Ministry Risk: Points to Consider," can assist you in getting a general impression of how risky the ministry is from a sexual abuse standpoint. Other questions and considerations might come to mind as you work your way through the list. Some teams have used this list to help them identify a number of ministries that have a high risk potential, without actually ranking them individually.

The second chart, figure 8.2, provides a method for assessing ministry risk using a simple checklist. Each one of the questions identifies a risky behavior. Each congregation needs to discuss these questions and decide what number of yeses will be allowed before the ministry will be considered risky and will be required to change the way the ministry is performed. I would suggest that if the answer to any of the questions is yes, that situation should be dealt with by immediately instituting appropriate procedures. The more yeses that are given for a particular ministry, the riskier it becomes.

CHOOSE A METHOD OF CONTROL

Evaluate the risks as they are identified. Which risks can your congregation tolerate? Which ones require the purchase of insurance? Which risks can be reduced? Which are simply too great to bear?

There are four ways to deal with the identified risks:

• *Avoid the risk*: Do not offer a service you consider too risky. Example: Decide not to offer day care because your church cannot meet the building code requirements of the state for fire safety and accessibility.

Risk Factor	Yes	No
Do one-to-one activities occur in isolated settings?		
Does volunteer minister operate without on-site supervision?		
Does volunteer minister role involve relationship(s) in which there is a power differential?		
Does volunteer minister develop one-on-one relationship with child or vulnerable adult as part of ministry?		
Could circumstances conceivably occur causing a child and provider of service to be left alone together?		
Does volunteer minister have physical contact with child or vulnerable adult in performance of ministry?		
Does volunteer minister interact with a specific child for long periods of time in one session or over a long span of time?		
Is there little or no parental or guardian involvement?		
Is access to confidential information involved?		
Does volunteer minister handle funds?		
Does volunteer minister have access to controlled substances?		
Does the ministry involve changing of clothes, bathing, or overnight stays?		
Is providing transportation involved?		
Is there a high turnover of staff and/or volunteer ministers?		
Are volunteer ministers permitted to receive gifts or gratuities of nominal value from client or family?		

Figure 8.2. Assessing Ministry Risk Checklist

- *Modify the risk*: Change the activity so that the chance of any harm occurring and the impact of the potential damage are acceptably low.
  Example: Hold all teen small-group meetings or classes at the church instead of in individuals' homes to lessen the chances of behavior that violates your policies.

- *Transfer the risk*: Find someone else to take on the risk on your behalf.
  Example: Contract with a bus company to take your youth group to an outing instead of relying on individual volunteer drivers. The bus company would have primary liability and insurance coverage for any accidents that might happen.

- *Retain the risk*: Continue with the activity after determining the risk is small enough that the congregation can sustain the loss if something happens.
  Example: Hold the teen marshmallow roast and sing-along, knowing that the fire can be closely supervised in an approved pit, teenagers are old enough to be able to handle hot forks with a minimum of supervision or danger to one another, and the church has liability insurance.

During this part of the preparation you should be in active dialog with leaders of the particular ministries on which you are focusing. The goal is to gain their full cooperation with any changes in procedures. This will be easier to achieve if you include them from the beginning by explaining why changes are important and *involving them in the planning* for any changes to how things are going to be done in their particular ministry.

RESEARCH AND CREATE POLICY

A policy should state that your parish has no tolerance for sexual abuse, define what is meant by sexual abuse, and state that it will cooperate with law enforcement agencies in investigating any allegations. Some of the issues a policy should address are these: what processes to follow in the event of an allegation of improper behavior, how the investigation will be handled and by whom, who will decide whether to notify police and what specific circumstances will influence that decision, how the alleged victim and perpetrator will be dealt with by the church during the course of the investigation, and if the perpetrator is found guilty through a legal process, consequences for the perpetrator regarding future participation in ministry work.

Many denominations and churches have written policies, so you probably will not have to start from scratch. Check with your own judicatory offices to see if they have a template to follow. If not, check with other churches in your denomination or neighborhood, or with contacts in nonprofit organizations, to gather examples of policies. I recommend that a small task force or subcommittee of the risk management committee be formed to write the policies and take them through the steps of approval. When the document is nearly finished, have a lawyer familiar with sexual abuse policies check the document for appropriate use of terminology from a legal standpoint.

Formally adopt the policies according to your church governing board's normal procedures. I also recommend that the senior pastor and the board chair sign the policy. The more signatures indicating official acceptance of the policy you have, the less likely you are to run into problems later.

Update and train paid staff regarding the policy prior to its rollout to the congregation. Each paid staff member's position description should state they will be expected to abide by all policies and procedures relating to protecting children and vulnerable adults. Some congregations require paid staff to sign and date a statement indicating that they have read and will follow the policy. The policy needs to then be introduced to the members of the congregation at large and especially to all members involved in ministry. Some congregations require volunteers in high-risk ministries to sign and date the same acknowledgment staff members sign.

This process of creating and approving the policy can take as long as a year. It can take even longer if the leadership first needs to be persuaded that policies and procedures are necessary. Policy making can be considered dull and dry stuff, but it is an essential element in your work to keep everyone safe.

PUT THE POLICY INTO EFFECT AND ENSURE COMPLIANCE

Creating a policy is not enough. There also needs to be some oversight and periodic evaluation of how well ministries are conforming to the policy. Establishing ways to train your staff and ministry members on the policies in general as well as the requirements for their specific ministries is an important element of risk management. There are many ways to accomplish the training. You can design a training class and present it to staff members and ministry leaders explaining the policies. A risk management manual can be written and given to staff and lay leaders. If you have been including lay leaders in the formulation of procedures, it should be a natural next step for them to introduce the procedures and explain the need for them to the ministry members they lead. Other steps to take are assisting ministries with editing their position descriptions so that they include required procedures and list screening requirements. Creating procedures, as covered below, will be part of that support structure.

CREATE OPERATING PROCEDURES

Procedures ensure that all ministries are conforming to the policies. They spell out exactly how people will implement the policies. These would include such things as screening requirements, such as interviewing and background checks; training requirements; supervision practices; reporting tools, such as incident reports; and how data will be collected and used to keep track of important information, such as the results from background checks.

You will do yourself a favor if you include representatives from each ministry with children and vulnerable adults as you plan what procedures need to be put in place for that ministry. Who better knows how things work now and what kind of potential danger should be dealt with? Staff members and lay leaders may also have efficient and effective ideas for coping with perceived risks in their situation. Their suggestions may provide you with ready-made procedures to deal with these risks. By including staff and lay leaders for the particular ministry, you increase the likelihood that they will support changes, and you have the benefit of their suggestions for creating procedures, which will save you time and effort.

You should have some general rules about numbers and ages of teachers and chaperones required to be present with any group of children, including in nurseries and classrooms and for overnight and camping-related events. Two adults is the minimum standard at this time, regardless of how few children are present. This number can be increased proportionately, depending on the number of children and their ages.

Open-door policies for one-on-one meetings with children, teens, and vulnerable adults; procedures for changing diapers in nurseries and taking children to the bathroom; and cleanliness processes in day-care and nursery settings are among other procedures that need to be created. It is important to design safe processes for dropping off and picking up children for nursery, preschool, or other classes and events. Procedures should also be established to identify people approved to take children out of the nursery, and rules put in place about how many adults need to be present when children are serving in a particular ministry. The consequences of failure to conform to the screening procedures need also to be spelled out and followed. For example, if a procedure requires all adult chaperones to have completed a background check before performing their ministry, a consequence of failing to complete one would consist of not being allowed to accompany the youth group on the camping trip. It generally takes only one instance of noncompliance and the resulting consequence to keep the situation from being repeated.

Background Checks

All volunteer ministers who work with children and vulnerable adults should receive background checks. Practices vary widely among states and jurisdictions. Depending on where your church is located, you may need to submit requests to your county, state, or city law enforcement agency to be processed. It is wise to find out exactly what records will be checked. Some states will only process their own state records. Other governmental units do only local city or county records.

With the mobility of today's population, you will want to track records for the past six to seven locations where the individual has lived or specify the number of years records should be searched. Often local governmental agencies will charge a nominal fee. They also may have dedicated computers for public use that you can access to do your own searches. However, there are now many companies with which a congregation can contract to do a very thorough investigation for a reasonable price. They offer different levels of searches and will look at a number of sources for data besides just local jurisdictions. They can check motor vehicle department records as well. Generally speaking, with each background-check request, you must submit an official permission form signed within the previous twelve months by the individual whose records will be checked. Forms can be obtained from the agency or company doing the background check.

Negotiating with background check companies for the lowest possible cost can help keep this budget item to a reasonable level. If it is possible to join with other churches in your denomination or geographical area, you can often obtain a volume discount. Here again it is wise to do some research to find out the experiences of other churches in using a particular company. Ask the company for references from other churches. Find out what other congregations' costs were, to give you an idea of the range of costs you can anticipate. By all means, ask for the cost information in any case. This necessary procedure can be a significant item in the shared ministry budget, not to mention the annual budget for your congregation. But the cost will be negligible compared to the cost of having an incident of abuse to deal with.

Note that minors' records are not open to the public, so background checks are not going to help you in screening those under eighteen who might have a history of sexual abuse problems. Here is where supervision is critical. Many churches now require two references from a child's or teen's teachers, coaches, or employers as one way of screening. Many organizations require personal interviews, which are especially important when you don't have background checks to evaluate. Also, you need to put strict supervision rules into place to ensure that adults are always present when teens are working with children.

While many churches ask for references for adults, it can be almost impossible to get information or forms back from references, no matter how well they know the individual who has asked for the reference. Even churches that have instituted rigorous follow-up methods for receiving the references find that only about 40 to 50 percent come back. The amount of time and effort required to track and follow up on references, not to mention the dubious value of the information you get from them, appears to indicate that you are better off expending time and energy on other procedures, such as interviewing, doing background checks, and instituting good supervision practices.

Driving Records

Criminal background checks don't necessarily cover driving records. But to ensure that children and vulnerable adults are safe, it is wise to create a process for checking the driving records of all those who will transport vulnerable people on field trips, on errands, to doctor's visits, or for other events. Your state department of motor vehicles can provide you with these records, or they may be obtained by the background check company, if you use one.

Many churches now require credit checks for all staff members and volunteers who work with cash and checks, such as weekend collection counters, those who make deposits, staff or volunteer ministers with check-writing privileges, or those handling bookkeeping tasks.

DEVELOP POSITION DESCRIPTIONS

Position descriptions are an important tool for several reasons. They help volunteer ministers learn what the requirements of the position are and determine whether they can meet them. They define the boundaries and expectations of the position, acting as a guide for leaders to help them identify behaviors that could indicate problems or potential problems brewing. You can use the position description to supervise, mentor, and if necessary reassign the individual who is not behaving or performing acceptably.

The position descriptions should delineate the responsibilities as well as the skills and gifts necessary for carrying out the particular ministry. Position descriptions should also list all the screening requirements for the position and identify required orientation and training sessions.

Written Records

Keep written records of the screening processes you use, in case you later need to prove that you used appropriate diligence and care in screening people. Even an application form can act as a deterrent to individuals who assume they will get easy access to vulnerable populations by volunteering at your church or organization. Professionals dealing with perpetrators have stated that a good proportion of them will take the path of least resistance. Each requirement that you institute puts one more roadblock in place to discourage them from joining a high-risk ministry.

The following records need to be kept.

- All applications, permission forms, signed code-of-conduct forms (if required), and so forth
- Background-check reports
- Interview notes
- Supervisory notes
- References, if done
- Lists of people who have been through the screening process
- Lists of people who have had a background check done and the result of such a check
- Copies of the risk management policy, any changes, and the dates they were approved

- Copies of risk management procedures, any changes, and the dates they were instituted
- Incident reports; that is, documentation of all incidences of inappropriate behavior and cases in which someone was prohibited from working with children or vulnerable adults due to the results of a background check

Such documentation may be crucial in a legal case many years later. What records need to be kept? How? For how long? What about storage and confidentiality issues? All these questions need to be thought out and decided upon.

PUBLICIZE THE RISK MANAGEMENT POLICY

I mentioned above under researching and creating a policy that it is important to inform the paid staff members and lay boards about the policy early on in the process. Other segments of the congregation also need to learn about the new policies and procedures once they have been created and approved.

Informing Ministry Members

Regardless of the number of volunteer ministers involved in a particular ministry, it is wise to have a standard format for orienting every individual to the ministry, including the screening requirements and procedures to which they must adhere. Having such an outline, and using it each time any person begins work in the ministry, ensures that all pertinent information will be covered and in the same way for every volunteer.

Many congregations have training about sexual abuse that includes facts such as prevalence, effects on victims, necessity for screening procedures, what the required screening processes are, characteristic behaviors of perpetrators, and how to fill out incident reports.

Informing the Congregation at Large

Not only the volunteer ministers but also the entire congregation should learn about the institution of the written policies and procedures and recognize that they are intended to keep the vulnerable safe. Copies of the policy can be mailed or handed out to congregation members after a weekend service. It is always a good idea to have the pastor and a representative lay leader talk about the rationale behind creating the policy and procedures and to indicate that they solidly support the approved documents. This will make it clear that the entire risk management process has the full backing of leaders in the congregation and that it is not a pet idea of the shared ministry team and director, and therefore to be taken lightly.

Bulletin boards and the congregation's website can highlight the results of the policy team's work. The director of shared ministry or other staff people can make short presentations at fellowship gatherings or prior to the start of an adult education event. If you have new member classes, the policy can be given to the attendees as part of their orientation to the congregation.

REGULARLY REVIEW AND REVISE

The last of the nine risk management steps that we have been discussing is often omitted. You can easily lose sight of it in the midst of all the other considerations. It will be important to schedule regular reviews for your policies and procedures. Ministries are very fluid and can easily change how they function from year to year. Major responsibilities may be added or deleted. Small, seemingly unimportant changes in how the ministry is carried out may necessitate that new procedures be devised. Change can occur quickly, depending on current leadership and perceived need for the change. It is important to keep up to date with the changes ministries make in their procedures. You may need to revise certain procedures from time to time to accurately reflect what is going on in a given ministry or as new situations surface.

Working out all these procedures is a labor-intensive task. Personal contact between the director of shared ministry and a knowledgeable ministry representative will be important if you are having trouble achieving maximum compliance with the procedures. A personal visit indicates the importance of the issue. It also gives you the opportunity to explore reasons for the failure to comply and to correct misunderstandings. All that effort will be worth it in the end if even just one child or vulnerable adult is protected from abuse because of what you have done. This is one of those situations in which you can't prove the negative. You can't prove that a child was protected if a potential perpetrator is prevented from signing up for a ministry because of the screening processes you require. There will be no way of tracking what might have gone wrong. Nevertheless, remain firm in the requirements you create. They do dissuade people from taking advantage of situations and harming others.

Of course, there are no absolute guarantees that even with all the policies and procedures in place you will never have an instance of abuse take place in your church. People do slip in or become abusers with no warning signals. However, if you have done everything you possibly can to prevent abuse from taking place, no matter how traumatic the event that may occur, you will be able to live with the knowledge that you tried to do everything in your power to prevent it. Will you be able to live with yourself if you haven't?

NECESSITY OF ADMINISTRATIVE HELP

The director of shared ministry should logically and reasonably expect to have overall responsibility for creating and supervising these policies and procedures. However, the director should not single-handedly take care of all the record-keeping requirements.

Depending on the size of your congregation and the number of volunteer ministers engaged in high-risk ministries, the following tasks might be performed by knowledgeable, trustworthy volunteer ministers:

- Design a database tracking component for risk management.
- Enter application information into the database.
- File paper applications, permission forms, and so forth.
- Design orientation and other training courses.
- Present the training courses.
- Write policies and procedures.
- Submit background check requests electronically.
- Provide staff members and lay leaders with lists of ministers who have completed all the screening requirements.

DEVELOPING A COMPREHENSIVE RISK MANAGEMENT PROCESS

Creating a risk management component from the ground up can seem overwhelming. But a combination of short- and long-term strategies will help you to put a comprehensive process in place in an orderly fashion. You can begin to create some elements of a program relatively quickly and easily. Other items require a longer time frame.

Short-Term Strategies

Short-term strategies are those that can be completed within one or two years. These risk management strategies need to be dealt with as soon as possible, regardless of the status of the policy creation process. Begin immediately to create procedures for high-risk ministries. Collaborate with staff and lay leaders to do the following:

- Establish requirements for the number of adults-to-children ratios that must be followed in all ministry activities.
- Institute a two-adult rule as an absolute minimum for all class and small group activities.
- Set open-door requirements in all classrooms, meeting rooms, counseling spaces, and so forth, or have windows installed in all doors in these areas.
- Create procedures for background checks to be done for all adults working with children and vulnerable adults.

- Create supervision processes for all high-risk ministries.
- Require staff members or trained volunteer ministers to have personal interviews with all adults working in close relationships with children and teens prior to beginning their ministry work.
- Set up orientation opportunities for all affected volunteer ministers to learn of the new procedures and what the new supervision processes and requirements are.
- Continually update the general parish membership on the details and rationale for instituting these procedures as you complete them.

Long-Term Strategies

Simultaneously, you will want to start developing strategies that will take more time to complete but are as important as the short-term ones for keeping your church safe. Long-term strategies identify those tasks that will take three to four years to complete. Here is where recruiting help from volunteer ministers who have a special skill or interest in a particular task can move the process along more quickly. The director of shared ministry does not have to have expertise in all these areas. Relying on knowledgeable assistance from other congregation members will decrease the pressure on directors to complete all these time-consuming tasks themselves.

- Create the official risk management policy.
  - Form a task group as described above.
  - Obtain model policies from other churches.
  - Research any requirements and tools available from your denominational offices.
  - Draft the document; revise, review, finalize.
  - Get official approvals from your governing boards, councils, and pastor.
  - Publish the policy.

- Promote, educate, and sell the congregation, staff, ministry leaders, and ministry members about the need for this policy and for methods and procedures that will be used to carry out the policy after it is approved.
- Oversee the creation or modification of position descriptions for all volunteer minister positions in all high-risk ministries, including new screening and other requirements.
- Create orientation classes for all ministry members working in high-risk ministries, and review the new policy, position descriptions, and procedures as these become available.
- Create screening processes, including application forms, background checks, and interviewing.
- Build a system for tracking background checks, application forms, and fulfillment of other required paperwork and training.
- Build cooperation at all levels with this program through collaboration and sharing of information.

ISSUES IN OBTAINING COMPLIANCE

You may experience a number of compliance issues with staff members and shared ministers as you work on risk management policies and procedures. Here are several you may encounter and suggestions for how to deal with them.

Volunteer minister refuses to be screened. Make it clear that this is a requirement for serving in the position. This requirement should be stated in the position description. If the person is unwilling to cooperate with the screening requirement for any reason, let him know that he will not be able to minister in that specific position. Offer to work with him to find a different area where he can minister comfortably that doesn't have these requirements.

Volunteer minister consistently ignores risk management procedures and carries out the ministry in a nonapproved way. Arrange a meeting between the director of shared ministry, the volunteer minister, and her staff supervisor or ministry leader. Investigate the reason for the failure to follow procedures and institute additional training, supervision, and so forth. If all these methods fail, remove the volunteer from the ministry and redirect her to a less high-risk ministry area.

Staff member fails to enforce the procedures previously agreed upon. Have a private discussion with the staff person to try to determine the reason for the failure to abide by the procedure. If he remains determined to ignore the requirements, have a private consultation with the supervisor or the pastor to request backing on this and bringing his or her authority to bear on the situation.

Volunteer minister tries to make an end run around the screening requirements by pointing out her longstanding position in the congregation or friendship with the pastor or other key leader as a reason for exemption from the requirements. Explain that there can be no exceptions to the screening rules for anyone. Unpleasant as it may be, all must follow the procedures; otherwise they have no meaning. Request that the pastor or staff person back you on this requirement. Sometimes you will need to coach the pastor or staff person who has trouble dealing with this issue, suggesting he or she refers to the approved policies and procedures as "out of my hands" and explains that the director of shared ministry is the final decision maker. If compliance with policies and procedures is waived for certain people, you will have lost credibility with the membership. More importantly, you will also open the door for abuse to potentially occur. It will be difficult to insist that all need to follow the policies if any are exempted.

A particular ministry staff person or lay leader consistently fails to provide you with the required paperwork for completing screening requirements. If reminders and requests are ignored, and you have gone to the staff person's supervisor about the issue, you need to go to the highest authority (that is, the pastor or head of staff) and request that he or she make it clear that cooperating with the approved procedures and policies is not optional. This is a requirement for that staff member's position. While you as director of shared ministry may not have the ability to hire or fire other staff, it is important for you to document noncompliance and the measures you have taken to bring about compliance. Should there be any ramifications later, you can at least show that you did everything in your power to bring about compliance with the procedure in question.

THE ISSUE OF CONFIDENTIALITY

The volunteer ministers who are going through the application and screening process need to be assured that their personal information will be kept confidential, so it is important to ensure confidentiality in gathering and processing information. Such things as Social Security numbers, police records, and other personal information that they may provide or that is discovered from the background check process should be carefully protected from being shared with the general membership.

The entire congregation does not need to know that thirty years ago, when John Doe was twenty years old, he was arrested for drug possession, or that Susie Smith received a ticket last year for speeding. Depending on the situation, it may be important for a supervising staff member to know about the speeding ticket if Susie is applying to be a driver for teen events. But other parents and teens do not need this information as long as you have taken precautions to redirect Susie into a ministry that does not require driving, for example, or you have required that Susie receive no speeding tickets for a year or longer before allowing her to drive for the church.

Situations such as past drug use need to be evaluated on a case-by-case basis. How long ago did the event happen? Was addiction involved? Has the person received treatment for the addiction? How long has the person been straight? Did the person deal drugs, or was he only a user? What is the nature of the ministry they are applying for? Is it likely that the person is continuing to use drugs or could be looking for a place with access to young people to continue the dealing? You will want to find out the answers to these questions as you consider whether the volunteer is appropriate for the ministry she or he is applying for.

If in doubt about the appropriateness of a particular individual working with children, teens, or vulnerable adults, redirect the person into a less risky area of ministry. It is difficult to write procedures that will tell you what to do about every combination of facts and situations. Sometimes you have to rely on prudent judgment based on a thorough investigation of the matter. Asking a couple of trusted staff people to discuss the situation with you is always a good idea, however. Getting input from them will assist you in making a good decision when there are gray areas. The main concern should be protecting the vulnerable from harm and the church from potential risk, while at the same time respecting the individual's right to confidentiality regarding past mistakes as much as possible.

If the situation concerns actual abuse of a child or vulnerable adult, you need to be very sure that all steps are taken to protect the child or adult from this person. The minister needs to be closely supervised at all times. She must be prevented from participating in any ministries that offer any exposure to children, teens, or vulnerable adults. Those with a need to know, such as staff members, can be informed of the potential risk this person presents. Discussions and advice from law enforcement or other professionals familiar with perpetrators will be important.

If you have volunteer ministers entering sensitive information into a database, it is essential to limit who has access to this data. Background-check information should be entered by only one volunteer who has been thoroughly trained in the importance of respecting the privacy of individuals and who has signed a statement promising to maintain confidentiality. In smaller congregations, it may be best for the director of shared ministry or another staff member to enter this data him- or herself. Background check reports should be kept under lock and key, and databases should be password protected.

Finally, it is essential to document all situations that present gray areas or that deal with people who are known perpetrators, including what the investigation revealed, whom it was discussed with, and whether the individual was allowed to participate in the specific ministry.

HOW TO PROCEED WITH AN EXISTING RISK MANAGEMENT PROGRAM

If a congregation has a risk management program or some of the elements of a program in place, the best policy is to thoroughly review each of the risk management components discussed in this chapter to determine which ones exist and which are missing, incomplete, or need updating.

Some questions to ask include these: Is the component applied to all high-risk ministries or only to some of them? Have all ministries been examined comprehensively and rated according to a consistent standard to determine which ones are high risks? What are the current screening practices? What records are kept? Who is responsible, and what exactly do they do? Where are records kept and who has access to them? Is there a written policy regarding protecting children and vulnerable adults from sexual abuse? Are position descriptions up to date? Do they list screening and training requirements?

Once you have done a thorough investigation into the existing practices and requirements, you will be in a good position to determine what will need to be added, significantly changed, or tweaked and to set priorities for perfecting the system.

ROLES FOR THE SHARED MINISTRY TEAM AND DIRECTOR

It should be apparent by now that creating and supervising a comprehensive risk management policy will require one person with the ability and authority to handle many of the tasks involved. Due to their nature, a number of the tasks mentioned above cannot be handled by a volunteer ministry team. Such things as access to confidential information, authority to remove individuals from a ministry area, or the ability to call individual staff members to account for failure to follow procedures are examples.

What can the shared ministry team do? The shared ministry team can initiate the process. It has a role in creating the policy and recommending its approval. A team member who has the appropriate gifts or interest may sit on the policy-making team and contribute to its work. The shared ministry team can offer input regarding the many decisions that will need to be made in creating the process and structure. Members can be enthusiastic proponents within the congregation about the need to create a risk management policy and procedures. They can support the director of shared ministry in handling objections and barriers and do other problem solving. They can assist with preliminary research about the necessity for having a risk management policy, locate sample policies, and design publicity materials, important forms, and the database for tracking all-important information. The team can help create training modules and even present parts of or all the training.

What does the director of shared ministry do? Working with and maintaining highly confidential information, making difficult decisions regarding specific situations and individuals, exercising the authority to require compliance with procedures, and establishing relationships that encourage full cooperation from paid staff—all are sensitive matters that the director of shared ministry or some other professional, paid staff member should handle. It might be possible to divide these responsibilities among several paid staff or particularly trustworthy members of the church. However, the more people involved in exchanging pertinent confidential information, the more likely it is that some key pieces will be missed, to the later regret of everyone involved.

Unless the congregation is very small (under one hundred members), I believe risk management is one good example of the need for a professional, paid staff person—the shared ministry director—to deal with this important issue. The role of the director of shared ministry is to orchestrate the development of risk management policies and procedures; recruit a policy-writing committee; update and get input from the shared ministry committee on progress and general issues that arise; and collaborate with the shared ministry committee, paid staff, and pastor, as appropriate, in achieving compliance with the policy.

The director should be the center point for gathering information, assessing specific situations, and making knowledgeable decisions. This individual may not actually perform all the many duties required by the risk management plan. Reasonable delegation must also be factored in. But one individual must understand all the components of an effective system so that it can be kept running smoothly for the safety of all.

CHAPTER 9

Understanding the Place of Gifts in Shared Ministry

Throughout the preceding chapters I have often used the term *gifts*. For example, in the chapter on recruitment, I discussed assisting people with discovering their gifts for ministry and giving them the opportunity to use those gifts. In the chapter on appreciation I talked about many ways to show thankfulness for the gifts of the individual and to celebrate the gifts of the entire congregation. The training component seeks to grow the gifts of the individuals and make it possible for them to more effectively use their gifts.

Gifts is a theme woven consistently throughout the shared ministry system. A parish that pays attention to the gifts of its members will find a natural connection between shared ministry and gifts-based ministry. I often talk with leaders of congregations who want members to "use their gifts in performing ministry." They want to develop a gifts inventory, encourage every member to complete it, and conduct a gifts-discovery or spiritual gifts class. That is about as far as they have gotten with their thinking. If I introduce the shared ministry model and don't make a concerted effort to show how it does the very thing they are looking for (pointing out the connections and parallel language in great detail), they assume that I am not going to be able to meet their needs. I have even heard inexperienced directors of volunteer ministry say that their leaders looked briefly at the shared ministry concept but decided to concentrate on gifts instead! Gifts-based ministry and shared ministry are not mutually exclusive. They are one and the same. In fact, one could write a definition for gifts-based ministry that parallels the shared ministry definition. Here is one I have developed:

A gifts-based ministry system:

- calls forth from the assembly,
- brings into personal awareness,
- invites their use in ministry,
- matches with appropriate opportunities,
- nurtures and develops,
- affirms,
- appreciates,
- enables reflection on,
- and celebrates the GIFTS
- of every individual,
- for the building up of the kingdom of God in the world.[1]

Shared ministry is all about building a system based on encouraging and enabling all members of the congregation to use their gifts. It actually *is* a gifts-based system. In shared ministry, every effort is made to make sure people are given a chance to develop their gifts through orientation, ongoing training, and support from their leaders.

To better understand what I mean, try this exercise: Take the elements of the shared ministry system (recruitment, supervision, evaluation, and so forth) and compose a couple of sentences that describe what is meant by each of them, using *gifts* language. For example, you might say, "Recruitment consists of inviting congregation members to offer their gifts, skills, passions, and interests in service to the mission of our church." Recasting the shared ministry description using language about gifts will help you to understand and to explain to others how shared ministry supports the gifts theme in ministry.

Gifts and the Question of Terminology

Some congregations prefer to use the term *gifts-based ministry* or some similar phrase when they begin establishing the ministry. Some churches like to use the concept of discipleship, as in *gifts for discipleship*. *Stewardship* is another term frequently employed to name our responsibility to use the gifts we have been given. Other congregations focus on *spiritual gifts* as the basis for ministry in the church. Generally, the term *spiritual gifts* is used to refer to lists of gifts gleaned from several passages in the New Testament and inferred from Old Testament writings. The concept is that these gifts are bestowed on individuals by God to be used specifically in building up the church and assisting it in fulfilling its mission on earth. Another term that is sometimes employed when talking about spiritual gifts is *charisms*. Some congregations make a distinction between spiritual gifts and other talents, skills, or abilities people possess. Many denominations have spiritual gifts inventories available for use by their members, and several nondenominational publishers have developed similar inventories for a broader audience. These can also be adapted to fit the needs of the particular congregation.

My own preference is to use the term *shared ministry* to refer to the system that enables everyone to use their gifts. I use the term *gifts* in its widest possible sense. I see spiritual gifts as a subset of all the gifts God has given each person. All that comes from a totally good, totally loving God is intended to be used for good in the world. All our experiences, personality characteristics, family background, physical makeup, abilities, interests, passions, and motivations, arising from each person's unique constellation of gifts, are to be used as the hands and feet of God. Even our hurts, disappointments, weaknesses, and wounds can be used as gifts to widen our perspective, teach us patience, and encourage compassion for others.

Of course, ideally the focus and terminology used for a shared ministry system fit the theology of the particular congregation or denomination. Care should be taken to think through the implications of the language chosen. How does this terminology mesh with the theological beliefs and ways of talking about the role of believers in your church? Will it flow naturally from these theological beliefs? Will it add a new emphasis that will enrich understanding and invite more people into ministry in the long run? Is it a good tool to encourage people to participate more deeply in the ministry of the church? Is there commitment by the leaders to work toward this new understanding by consistently using the language selected? No matter what terminology you use, however, plan on building a system containing the essential elements discussed in earlier chapters.

Ways to Help People Discover Their Gifts for Ministry

Not every person understands what his or her gifts are. Often our gifts are so natural and integral to the way we live our lives that we assume everyone else has the same aptitudes. We don't identify them as gifts. Other people believe they have no gifts! Older generations may have been taught that to talk about their gifts is bragging. They learned that it is better to be humble, to deny gifts, bury them, or wait until others discover them, rather than to acknowledge them and risk being considered prideful by others. A variety of tools are available for assisting people with identifying their gifts for ministry and using them joyfully in service.

GIFTS-DISCOVERY CLASSES

Gifts-discovery classes can help participants raise their awareness of and identify personality traits, strengths, motivations, past experiences, sources of energy, calls to new challenges, actions that give one a sense of fulfillment and joy, and many other gifts. Many directors of shared ministry design their own classes. Shared ministry team members can be an excellent source of ideas, write lesson plans, and assist with hospitality and training.

Another valuable resource for designing gifts-discovery classes is a book by Jean Trumbauer, *Created and Called*.[2] This manual provides many reproducible exercises to use in such classes. A table in the book categorizes exercises according to the length of time needed to complete the reflection and suggested uses, such as brief community builders at meetings, training for volunteer ministers, leadership retreat days, and so forth. You can find other suggestions and tools by scanning the Web and investigating denominational resources.

GIFTS-DISCOVERY INTERVIEWS

Gifts-discovery interviews are structured, one-on-one discussions held privately with individuals to delve into their experiences, interests, hobbies, previous volunteer involvements, and other such topics. The interviewer's goal is to get to know the individual well enough to suggest ministry opportunities that might make the best use of the person's available time, gifts, and interests. A skilled interviewer will focus completely on the person being interviewed. She or he will encourage the person to share his story in as much detail as he chooses, recognizing that it is a great gift for an individual to be given a chance to talk to a sympathetic person for an entire hour, with the focus just on him.

This tool addresses a problem that can arise from relying on a gifts-discovery class alone. Often people cannot make the leap from identifying their gifts to connecting them to the wide range of opportunities that may be available in your parish. During the discussion, the purposes and position expectations for various ministries can be more fully laid out for the individual. If the person expresses interest in a particular ministry, the interviewer can make the first connections with ministry leaders or provide contact information to the interviewee.

Sometimes it becomes clear through the interview that the individual is already overloaded with responsibilities, family needs, job challenges, health issues, or other demands on his or her time and energy. In some cases I have had to encourage the person I was interviewing to slow down and *not* get involved in any ministry work for now. Yet often these extremely conscientious people feel they ought to be volunteering in their church community on top of an already very difficult schedule. The interviewer can give permission to busy people to lay aside their volunteer work and to attend to the more pressing commitments in their lives. God does not expect the impossible from us. The interviewer might also suggest that overtaxed people are being called to employ little-used gifts in the situation at hand and that they can take up their accustomed gifts and passions to join in ministry in their congregation in another season. The message the church should be giving is that when people are dealing with difficult circumstances, it is okay to defer serving for a while. The congregation stands ready to welcome the person back into ministry when the time is right. In situations like these, the interview becomes more about what the congregation can do for the individual rather than what gifts the individual can bring to the congregation.

GIFTS INVENTORIES

A gifts inventory is a list of possible gifts, interests, and skills. The individual checks off which ones he or she has. These inventories work best for people who have a pretty good idea of their skills and interests. People who are struggling to identify their gifts often benefit from taking a gifts interview or gifts-discovery class before filling in a gifts-inventory form.

Gifts inventories may be short and simple or long and sophisticated. They can ask for other information besides gifts, such as months or times of day when people are available, preferred length of commitment, work styles, and so forth. The information is entered into a database, a gifts bank, for future reference. The database can be sorted to find all people who possess the gifts a ministry is looking for. Typically the director of shared ministry would provide the ministry leader or staff person with a list of candidates, who would then be sent targeted invitations.

Gifts inventories present several challenges. First, obtaining a large enough pool of completed inventories can be difficult, especially when the concept of shared ministry is new to a congregation. Another challenge is assisting the particular ministry in identifying the specific gifts they are looking for so that a database search will give them good results. In addition, the language used in a published inventory might not fit your congregation's theology. Even if a gifts-discovery inventory generally suits your congregation's needs, you still might need to adapt it to fit your congregation's particular theology.

A gifts inventory is not to be confused with a recruitment form. People complete a recruitment form when signing up to work in a specific ministry or perform a specific task. They fill out a gifts inventory to share information about gifts they believe they possess. It is important for those filling out a gifts inventory to understand that, based on those gifts, an invitation *may* be issued to participate in a particular ministry—one that fits the individual's gifts. But the person always has the option of declining the invitation. When the individual fills out a gifts inventory, he or she is not signing up to participate in any specific ministry. People often confuse the purpose of a gifts inventory. They then feel disappointed when they are not immediately contacted and invited to join a ministry.

A Caveat

The concept of gifts-based ministry is often an exciting and motivating one for shared ministry teams and leaders. It is an excellent way to present the idea that each congregation member can become involved in ministry. But by itself it is not a magical solution to a congregation's problems.

Sometimes I have seen a pastor and leadership group take hold of the gifts-discovery part of shared ministry but disregard all the other system building that has to accompany this in order for shared ministry to take hold in a congregation. They plan a gifts-discovery workshop and work up a gifts inventory for participants to use. They put all their hopes on this class or inventory and then are discouraged when it doesn't take them where they want to go—all because they haven't taken the time to build the underlying support structure. After the first blush of success, when people attend the gifts class or fill out the inventory, the momentum grinds to a halt. Where to go from here? It appears to the leaders that while gifts-based ministry is an intriguing idea, it doesn't infuse a majority of the congregation with energy for participating in ministry.

Leaders tend to forget that although people will get excited about gifts-based ministry, not everyone in the faith community is going to participate in a gifts class, participate in an interview, or complete an inventory. People have to be at the right point in their lives to be open to, interested in, and able to attend a gifts class or even reflect on their gifts. Gifts discovery is not for everyone. Those who do participate in gifts discovery will have been exposed to this new way of looking at church membership and may become active ministry members as a result. The rest of the congregation will likely remain in the dark, however, if gifts discovery is the only shared ministry component a congregation develops. Furthermore, even people who have reflected on their gifts for ministry, or simply have a good grasp of what gifts they possess, might take quite a while to integrate what they know about their gifts with their understanding of what their gifts mean for their participation in their congregation and the enrichment of their spiritual lives. Achieving this integration requires time and energy.

From a strategic standpoint, all the gifts-based ministry tools discussed above can be worked on in the background if skilled leaders are passionate about them and want to organize the effort. For a first-time event, however, you will get better results by focusing first on other components. Individuals' learnings from gifts-discovery classes or other experiences will have lower visibility in the congregation than, for example, a parish-wide recruitment event or a celebration of the gifts of the entire membership. It is wise to choose as a first initiative something that will give you visible and quantifiable results. A more visible project alerts more of the congregation that something new is going on. This will give the shared ministry team momentum and increase support for other projects.

For these reasons I usually advise congregations to wait until they have developed other elements of shared ministry like planning, recruitment, follow-up procedures, a method for thanking members for their contributions to the mission of the church, and a good start on the risk management component. Once these efforts are well under way, the gifts-discovery component can be helpful for attracting into ministry new members who need more assistance identifying their gifts. Gifts-discovery classes or interviews can also be an excellent way for experienced ministers to evaluate their volunteer work and choose new areas to participate in.

If the congregation has people passionate about working on gifts classes, interviewing, and gifts inventories, an option would be to recruit those ministers to a separate team to concentrate on the gifts aspect, while the shared ministry team builds the other elements of the system. This approach takes intense coordination, however, so that the two teams are not operating as if they were developing separate cultures. To make this option work requires enough people resources to cover both gifts-based and structural components. The director must be able to train and support ministers in two major thrusts simultaneously. Both aspects of shared ministry must be presented to the congregation as elements of a single emphasis.

Gifts discovery is an intriguing part of the total shared ministry system. Watching people respond to the idea that they are indeed gifted and that their gifts are valuable in helping the church to accomplish its mission is very rewarding. Even though a small number of people may participate in a gifts-discovery class, each one grows in self-understanding, a fascinating process to watch. Personal interviews allow the interviewer to work one-on-one with individuals, often a gratifying experience. No matter what gifts-discovery methods a congregation uses, however, shared ministry leaders have an opportunity to see the fruit of their work, as individuals join ministries and become involved members of the congregation. Individuals serve with a great sense of joy rather than a sense of duty. In addition, individuals' increasing awareness of their gifts often causes new ministries to spring up. Speaking from personal experience, I can attest that watching these changes take place in a congregation is one of the most satisfying experiences a shared ministry leader can have.

CHAPTER 10

Putting the Pieces Together

B uilding a shared ministry culture in a congregation is a fascinating and challenging task. Imagine you have in your hands
a large box containing many hundreds of puzzle pieces. You dump
the box over and watch all the pieces fall and scatter across the
table. This is what congregational life looks like when you begin
the process of building a shared ministry system. The task can
seem overwhelming. But here is where the benefits of training the
shared ministry team and staff person come in.

An introductory training can help your team become familiar
with the major steps in building a shared ministry system. From
there, if the team puts together a two-year plan, for example, they
will understand which parts of the puzzle to emphasize. Perhaps
one goal is to hold a recruitment event at the conclusion of the
two years. As planning takes place, it becomes apparent from their
training that position descriptions must be developed for the recruitment event. Or, using the analogy, it becomes evident from
studying the picture of the puzzle on the front of the box—say, a
bucolic rural scene—that completing the tree portion of the puzzle
will automatically aid in filling in the pieces of the sky around it.

As you look more closely at the chaos on the table, you also
begin to notice that some pieces have remained joined together.
There are two pieces here, three or four there. Think of these as
system components of ministries that are already functioning well.
One ministry, through experience, may have found that a good
training process is essential. Another ministry has an adequate

recruitment process and does a good yearly evaluation designed to continue to improve its work.

You also notice in a couple of places fairly large clumps of connected puzzle pieces that did not come apart in the fall from the box. Think of these clumps as representing multiple shared ministry components from entire ministry areas, such as the justice and charity area, for example. The food shelf team, groups that work with Feed My Starving Children, Habitat for Humanity, immigrant advocacy, and so forth all share a common goal of assisting the needy and changing unjust systems. They all have established, uniform methods for carrying out numerous system components. Thus, they are clumped together in the puzzle. They each contribute similar pieces to specific areas of the puzzle.

From experience, you know that one side of each puzzle piece is printed with a small section of the entire puzzle. All are a necessary part of the full picture. Similarly, there already exists in any congregation an underlying culture that connects all the various ministries, groups, relationships, and operations in this faith community The congregation is not a blank slate. Some connections are stronger than others. Some groups—individual puzzle pieces—seemingly operate on their own. Groups of ministries—those clumps of puzzle pieces—are already connected through their development of shared ministry components. Other puzzle pieces that need to be connected to each other to successfully complete the picture haven't yet been attached in their correct positions. But all are essential to building a completed organization or picture.

Your job is to assist the congregation in putting as much of the puzzle together as possible, thereby contributing to more effective and satisfying ministry. So you build the puzzle a component at a time. One day you may discover a missing corner piece. Rejoice! Here is something to anchor the rest of the puzzle to over time. Another day you spend many hours searching and discover only a couple of pieces that go together. A third day you may work on linking several more pieces together. While working on building that annual recruitment event you are interrupted by a call from a ministry leader who wants advice about how to show appreciation for the members of her team. Aha! Here's another opportunity to work on a different puzzle component.

Rarely will you be able to methodically build an entire section of the puzzle all at once. Each day you will add more and more individual pieces, some here and some there. While you may be concentrating on a particular area of the puzzle, say the roof of a house, and while you are always on the lookout for matching brown components of the puzzle, you also need to attend to puzzle pieces that belong in the sky, a flower bed, and the flowing stream. Then an unexpected opportunity will arise for you to add a puzzle piece to a tree, so you work on that for a while. The challenge is keeping the whole picture in your head while working on just small components here and there. The joy comes every time you fit another puzzle piece into the whole.

When you work on a puzzle, the work is slow going at the beginning. If the puzzle is especially large, the task may seem overwhelming. You put in lots of hours just to locate one piece, and even then, you might just let it sit on the table for a time in the general area where it seems to belong, even though you cannot yet connect it to any other pieces. As you work, you might think of the planning you have done at the outset as the picture on the front of the box. It shows you what the completed puzzle will look like. If there were no picture, the task would become too frustrating to attempt. Without a plan and idea of where you are heading, it is easy to get overwhelmed.

As time passes, however, and more puzzle pieces are put together, a certain momentum begins to build. There are fewer open spaces to fill in, more puzzle pieces can be found more quickly and settled into their correct spots. Similarly, as the shared ministry culture becomes more apparent, others see the connections and can imagine what the final picture will look like. So they gain energy and motivation to assist with putting it all together. No longer do only the shared ministry director and team know what the final picture will look like; many others catch the vision. Excitement builds. When you reach this point in the process, many days bring delightful new achievements and surprises. But at the beginning, things take much more effort, and the rewards are fewer and farther between. So it is wise to take the long view and remind yourself that for quite a while, you will be putting one piece in the puzzle at a time. Even getting that one piece in place may take a sustained effort over many months.

Here is where faith in God's guidance and belief in the value of what you are doing and in the power of the system you are building is important. This trust will give you the staying power you will need to continue when progress seems so slow. Sharing your dreams, plans, and successes as well as the challenges with a team of people will also give you the needed support for the work before you.

There are rewards along the way. A volunteer minister spontaneously remarks, "I just love what I am doing!" The number of recruitment forms returned steadily increases each year. A staff member, lay ministry leader, or particular ministry area catches on to the idea of thanking volunteer ministers. A youth ministry leader comes to you and asks what she can do to screen volunteers for their ministry area. Some of these are seemingly small victories, but every single one adds more pieces to complete the puzzle, that is, to build the culture. Recognize them, and rejoice when they come your way.

Conclusion

Though I have tried to keep the material in this book simple, you undoubtedly realize that building a shared ministry culture is a complex undertaking. What I hope the book has done for you is to create a pathway through some of the start-up processes. I have tried to explain what the big picture looks like and how to go about creating the most important elements. Rather than just listing a series of broad steps, I have tried to share the benefits of my experience by digging into the details. My hope is that you are feeling better equipped to change the culture of your congregation more efficiently and quickly.

Over time you and the team can move on to other elements besides the ones covered in this book. These include shared ministry system components such as designing ministries, matching, training, supervising, and evaluating. There are always opportunities to embellish the existing processes as well. Times change. People change. Ministries change. Lay leadership evolves, and staff members come and go. Trends in the larger society affect how each ministry does its work. Constantly evolving circumstances will challenge you to restructure and create new processes over the years.

I believe that congregations need to grow a shared ministry culture in order to adequately address the challenges of the future. Our world is crying out for gifts and passions that have been too long ignored. Name a troublesome issue your parish is dealing with or that is on the horizon. Chances are some elements of the shared ministry system can enable you to address those difficulties or even avoid them all together. As the faith community gets better at inviting and using the gifts of God's people, it brings ministry members into closer union with the Creator. How wonderful it is to play a part in such an endeavor.

Suggested Resources

Chand, Samuel R. *Cracking Your Church's Culture: Seven Keys to Unleashing Vision and Inspiration*. San Francisco: Jossey-Bass, 2011.

Chand describes five church cultures (inspiring, accepting, stagnant, discouraging, toxic) and ways to identify the particular strengths and needs of your church's culture. He presents seven keys of CULTURE (control, understanding, leadership, trust, unafraid, responsive, and execution) that will assist in creating a culture in which people are stimulated to do their best and reach their highest goals.

Hybels, Bill. *The Volunteer Revolution: Unleashing the Power of Everybody*. Grand Rapids: Zondervan, 2004.

Addressed to volunteers themselves, this book casts a vision of what a congregation would look like if everybody was serving using their God-given talents and passions. Through stories and straightforward advice, the author describes how volunteers can join in God's mission to change the world for the better.

Mallory, Sue, and Brad Smith. *The Equipping Church Guidebook*. Grand Rapids: Zondervan, 2001.

An excellent book for taking congregation leaders through the step-by-step planning process for building a "healthy equipping ministry," this manual helps readers lay relational and strategic foundations and build on them to create an effective and engaging volunteer ministry system.

Trumbauer, Jean Morris. *Created and Called: Discovering Our Gifts for Abundant Living.* Minneapolis: Augsburg Fortress, 1998.
This manual provides a multitude of resources to support comprehensive gifts ministry in Protestant and Catholic congregations. From an extensive chapter on the theology of gifts to sections on facilitating gifts seminars; discussions on broad categories such as gifts of style, traditional gifts, and gifts of vulnerability; sample gifts inventories; church models; and many reproducible pages, this book is a primer on developing gifts ministry in your congregation.

———. *Sharing the Ministry: A Practical Guide for Transforming Volunteers into Ministers.* Minneapolis: Augsburg Fortress, 1995.
This book remains the standard for developing a shared ministry system in congregations. It covers the components of such a system: planning, gifts discovery, designing ministries, recruitment, interviewing, matching, training, support, supervision, evaluation, and managing data. There are many reproducible pages with helpful examples of templates, handouts, and guides.

Vineyard, Sue. *The Great Trainer's Guide: How to Train (Almost) Anyone to Do (Almost) Anything!* Downers Grove, IL: Heritage Arts Publishing, 1990.
Using both prose and checklists, this book brings theories of educating adults to readers with easy-to-understand, real-life discussions and examples, including touches of humor and amusing graphics. A great resource for anyone struggling to learn how to train adults for ministry.

Web Resources

Church Volunteer Central (ChurchVolunteerCentral.com)
A resource developed by Group Publishing, this website provides short online courses about best practices for building

volunteer systems in congregations, as well as networking opportunities. Users must join to obtain access to all the resources it provides.

Directors of Church Volunteer Ministries (DCVM.org)

This faith-based network is under the umbrella of Minnesota Association of Volunteer Associations (MAVA, below). Individuals who direct volunteer programs in churches and congregations, and those who have an interest in the topic, will find many practical resources, networking opportunities, notices about regular retreats, and a job bank. Participation is free with membership in MAVA.

Minnesota Association for Volunteer Administration (mavanetwork.org)

The website for the Minnesota state organization of volunteer managers is filled with resources, educational opportunities, and informative articles relating to the profession and best practices. Site users must join the organization to gain access to all its features.

Notes

PREFACE

1. Jean Morris Trumbauer, *Sharing the Ministry: A Practical Guide for Transforming Volunteers into Ministers* (Minneapolis: Augsburg Fortress, 1995).

CHAPTER 1: WHAT IS SHARED MINISTRY ANYWAY?

1. Jean Morris Trumbauer, *Sharing the Ministry: A Practical Guide for Transforming Volunteers into Ministers* (Minneapolis: Augsburg Fortress, 1995).
2. Ibid., 50.
3. This term was used by Jean Morris Trumbauer in her book *Created and Called: Discovering Our Gifts for Abundant Living* (Minneapolis: Augsburg Fortress, 1998), 44, 52.
4. Trumbauer, *Sharing the Ministry*, 31.

CHAPTER 5: TAKING THE FIRST STEPS

1. For an example of a state association for directors of volunteers in nonprofit and faith-based organizations, visit the website of the Minnesota Association for Volunteer Administrations (MAVA), www.mavanetwork.org. For information regarding an ecumenical group of faith-based directors of volunteer ministers, see DCVM.org, which also can be found as a link from the MAVA website.

CHAPTER 6: DOING A CHURCHWIDE RECRUITMENT DRIVE

1. I have adapted this format from one used by Jean Trumbauer.
2. I am indebted to Jean Trumbauer for her ideas on uses for position descriptions.

3. I would like to thank Plymouth Congregational Church, Minneapolis, MN, for sharing this early version of a ministry sign-up form.
4. I am indebted to the Church of St. John Neumann, Eagan, MN, and Barb Orzechowski, Pastoral Associate for Shared Ministry, for allowing me to use parts of their ministry recruitment booklet and sign-up sheet.
5. This example is also provided by St. John Neumann Church.

CHAPTER 8: KEEPING EVERYBODY SAFE

1. Charles Tremper and Gwynne Kostin, *No Surprises: Controlling Risks in Volunteer Programs* (Washington, DC: Nonprofit Risk Management Center, 1993), 5.
2. James F. Cobble Jr., Richard R. Hammar, and Steven W. Klipowicz, *Reducing the Risk II: Making Your Church Safe from Child Sexual Abuse* (Matthews, NC: Christian Ministry Resources, 2003). Composed of a kit containing Training DVD, Leader's Guide, Trainee Workbook, and other resources. For more details see the website: www.reducingtherisk.com.

CHAPTER 9: UNDERSTANDING THE PLACE OF GIFTS IN SHARED MINISTRY

1. I understand that copyright law grants people the right to quote my definition. I hope that if you choose to do so, you will credit me for it.
2. Jean Morris Trumbauer, *Created and Called: Discovering Our Gifts for Abundant Living* (Minneapolis: Augsburg Fortress, 1998).